Exegetical Analysis

of

THE EPISTLES

With Notes

by

Isaiah B. Grubbs

Professor of Sacred Literature in the College of the Bible
Kentucky University

ISBN 1-58427-074-8

Guardian of Truth Foundation
P.O. Box 9670
Bowling Green, Kentucky 42102

PREFACE.

To assume that the exegetical analysis given in this treatise is faultless, or that the answers to queries is beyond the corrective power of wholesome criticism is to entertain a presumptuous feeling of which the author holds himself to be absolutely incapable. Infinitely better than any pretension to infallibility is the sincere effort made therein to act constantly under the guidance and regulation of the laws of Hermeneutics which must be observed by all who would interpret the Scriptures correctly. As with his classes in College, so with the readers of this work, the author insists on the subjection of every exposition to the rigid application of the fixed principles of interpretation and the acceptance of nothing on the mere authority of any exegete. It is the usual method in Universities, both in the old world and the new, for a learned professor of exegesis to pour out in lectures before his pupils the results of his own investigations and require recitations from notes on the matters presented. Students will neither acquire the habit of applying with facility the principles of Hermeneutics by this mode of procedure nor be afforded the opportunity of developing the power of thought and of testing, under the guidance of this important science, the merits of the exegesis submitted. There is a sort of idolatrous worship offered at the shrine of scholarship that greatly interferes with mental independence in interpretation and the ready acceptance of conclusions that may be fully justified by the principles applicable in the case apart from the mere approbation of learned expositors. Exegetes should be consulted as aids and not quoted as authorities whatever may be their learning or the weight of their names. Their interpretations must be freely examined in the true light of our science under a severe application of its principles and the legitimate result accepted without hesitation. The unreasonable reverence for great names and the idolatry offered to learning which is so exceedingly prevalent must be abandoned and all expositions be allowed to stand or fall just as they may, or may not, abide the only scientific test by which their merits may be determined.

Scholars can be partisans as well as others and the religious world is full of errors that are more or less blindly accepted as harmonious with the Holy Scriptures because human learning in giving them its sanction is regarded as demonstrative of their correctness. Let us, in exegesis at least, proceed on the basis of scientific principles, yet willingly and modestly accept any aid that the learned and thoughtful may legitimately extend to us in our work. And if any one on reading this treatise exercises the unquestioned right to dissent from any given exposition let him justify his dissent under the application of the laws of Hermeneutics or exchange it for approbation by the same appropriate test.

I. B. GRUBBS.

Lexington, Ky.

BIBLICAL HERMENEUTICS.

DEFINITIONS AND DISTINCTIONS.

1. Hermeneutics is the science of interpretation, and Exegesis is the practical application of the principles of this science in ascertaining or in setting forth the meaning of a passage or a statement. These principles are founded on the laws of thought as related to verbal usage and find their justification in the dictates of common sense.

2. As conclusions in mathematics can derive no force from the authority of mathematicians, since all that is truly scientific is independent of such authority, so the results of exegesis conducted under the faithful application of the laws of Hermeneutics must be received without reference to any supposed authority of exegetes. An authoritative expositor is as needless as an authoritative chemist, except in the case of inspired exposition of what had been previously only partially revealed. It follows that Hermeneutics as a science, embracing fixed principles that are founded on common sense, effectually excludes all claims to the office of authoritative or infallible interpretation for mankind.

3. It will follow with equal certainty that the right of private or individual interpretation involves no license to pursue fancies in exegesis, no freedom from the control or wholesome guidance of laws that do not vary, but the liberty to follow this scientific leading to legitimate results apart from dogmatic dictation from any source. When the claim to establish an authoritative standard in exposition is urged as necessary to prevent unlimited variation or wild extravagance in interpretation, it is clear that both the unwarranted claim and the argument for its supposed necessity are alike based upon the false assumption that there is

no science of Hermeneutics.   As a science with laws to be strictly
observed in interpretation, Hermeneutics stands equally opposed
to authoritative dictation, on the one hand, and to lawless exegesis, on the other.

4. The Author of revealed truth, indisputably intending to be
understood, has so embodied in expressions of this truth the meaning to be thus imparted for the benefit of mankind, that nothing
but a false exegesis involving the neglect or the deliberate repudiation of the principles of Hermeneutics can obscure the true sense
of the divine word. He who sets forth this divine sense of Sacred
Scripture presents no mere interpretation but that which, existing
apart from all exegesis, may nevertheless be readily perceived
under a thoughtful and faithful application of those laws of interpretation which common sense approves and which can never with
safety or propriety be disregarded by any exegete.

5. Biblical Hermeneutics, in short, simply brings the earnest
interpreter to a position on which the light of divine truth is allowed
to fall in all the fulness and clearness of its own teaching.   Its
testimony on any subject, whether given in one place or in several, must be taken in its entirety without abridgment or modification, so that the Holy Scriptures may interpret themselves in the
broad clear light of their own divine teaching.   And what we
call the laws of interpretation are simply certain sensible directions
to be followed as indispensable for bringing the learning mind
of man into uninterrupted contact with the instructing mind of
God.

SUBJECTIVE CONDITIONS.

6. It is needful that the interpreter of the Scriptures should not
only submit to the guidance of Hermeneutical laws but that he
also should approach the divine word in certain states of mind
that are conditional to his success.   A *special capacity* by nature
for the highest success in this as in other lines of study is an important prerequisite.   *Discipline* through study and exegetical exercise will in some measure increase this capacity, and thus propor-
tionately qualify those whom nature has not so well adapted to
this work.   In all cases *freedom*, from the bias of prejudice, partisan feeling and prepossession of every kind, is absolutely indispensable. This Hermeneutical freedom is exceedingly comprehensive.

It is, in the first place, freedom from all intellectual prepossessions. It is, in the second place, freedom from every moral bias, such as a lack of candor or sincerity. And the interpreter must not only be free from the dogmatism of others, but must especially be exempt from all dogmatism of his own.

7. These mental qualifications of the interpreter, or subjective conditions of reliable exegesis, deserve additional explanation and emphasis. The specific Hermeneutical capacity embraces three leading elements : discriminating ability, analytical power, and logical acumen. Sharpness of discrimination is necessary and lack of this power would hinder the process of a true interpretation. Interpreters should correctly distinguish between the ideas embodied in expressions that may closely resemble each other in form yet differ essentially in significance. Much of Holy Scripture is given in the form of reasoning, and a failure to grasp clearly the connection between premises and conclusion will interrupt the process of satisfactory interpretation. The cultivation of the powers to which reference is here made, in as high degree as possible, will render correct exegesis the more easy and delightful. Such an interpreter, applying faithfully the principles of Hermeneutics, in full possession of intellectual freedom and sincerity with himself and with his God, will find the divine word to be not only intelligible, but so convincing as to dispel the darkness of unbelief.

VERBAL CANONS.

8. Among the principles indispensable to the safe guidance of the interpreter there are certain canons of usage that may be said to partake largely of the nature of axioms. (*1*). *A word of more than one meaning may be properly used either affirmatively or negatively in a given proposition, while a word of only one meaning cannot be so used without contradiction.* Thus Paul teaches us that men are justified, "without works," Rom. iv. 5, while James us clearly affirms that men are justified, "by works." Each apostle furnishes the ground on which the harmony of the two may be seen. Paul speaks of "works" by which "faith is made void," Rom. iv. 14, and James speaks of "works" by which faith is "made perfect." Jas. ii. 22. When Luther discovered a difference of meaning in their use of the term "works," he no longer spoke of the Epistle of James as "an epistle of straw."

9. (2). Whatever may be the varieties of meaning a word may have in different connections, it can have but one import in any given instance of its occurrence. When Jesus said to unconverted Jews, Jno. v. 40, "ye will not come to me, that ye may have life," he could just as truly have said, according to Rom. viii. 6, you have no life, no spirituality of mind or renewal of heart, that you may come unto me. The latter is the condition of coming to him while the former is conditioned on coming. The life antecedent to coming is subjective life or spiritual renewal. The life that is consequent on coming is the objective bestowment of salvation through remission of sins. And it is obvious that the life which is the consequent of coming to Jesus can never be the antecedent condition of coming, nor *vice versa*. The word "life" cannot signify both in any given instance of its occurrence. In like manner a conjunction or a preposition, connecting several antecedent conditions with a consequent blessing, cannot denote any difference of relation in the case.

10. (3). Words, unlike numerals, may be used with a greater or a less comprehensiveness of import by virtue of their connection with other words. In no combination of numbers does the numeral 5 ever expand in value to 6 or, by contraction, become equal to 4. But words are susceptible in some measure of expansion and contraction in force, according to the connection in which they may be used. The word "righteous" is used with far greater comprehensiveness in Luke i. 6 and similar instances, than the measure of its import in Rom. v. 7 and in many other places of its occurrence. The *carnal màn*, as described in Rom. viii. 5-8, is the godless man, as standing in full contrast with children of God; but this term is applied with less meaning, of course, to believing "babes in Christ" in I. Cor. iii. 1.   And the word is still further contracted in force when applied by Paul to himself, Rom. vii. 14, under a comparison with the faultless law of God. It is one of the chief sources of erroneous exegesis that men adopt a sort of arithmetical method of interpretation, and deal with words as if they were numerals, in overlooking the obvious contextual import which they often acquire.

11. (4). This property inherent in words follows of necessity a correct translation or definition so that the latter can take the place of the former without detriment to the sense. In this way may be tested the merits or demerits of a definition or translation. The name Jesus means Saviour and as Jesus the Nazarene is emphatically the one only Saviour of men, to say that Jesus came into the world to redeem mankind is to say that our Saviour did this.

12. (5). *All words are susceptible of a figurative application, but no word has properly a figurative meaning.* No lexicographer would think of extending the signification of the word "fox" so as to include one of the Herodian family. When, in reference to Herod the tetrarch Jesus said to certain Pharisees, "Go and say to that fox," etc., he simply made a *figurative application* of this term to Herod, because of his resemblance in certain respects to the animal denoted by that word. So too, when by the figure of speech called *Metonymy, the name of an act is transferred to its effect*, as when an object ceremonially unclean was said to be sprinkled from its uncleanness, referring to the purification effected by this act, we have only a *figurative use* of the word "sprinkle" with no change of meaning whatever *in relation to the act* universally expressed by the term. Even when the figurative application is pushed still further into the realm of the spiritual, as in the expression, "having our hearts sprinkled from an evil conscience," *the meaning of the word*, as denoting a certain act, remains without modification.

13. (6). *As the words of a living language are constantly liable to change of meaning, a figurative application of frequent occurrence may gradually become the current meaning of a word and the original import become obsolete.* The expression *to prevent* formerly meant, according to its etymology, *to come before*, and so, by consequence, *to hinder*. The latter is at present the current import of the term, while the former has become obsolete. Usage may effect a change of signification through the influence of a variety of causes. "Great care therefore," says Ernesti, "is necessary in the interpreter to guard against rash etymological exegesis, which is often very fallacious. Etymology often belongs rather to the history of language than to the illustration of its present meaning, and rarely does it exhibit anything more than a specious illustration." Usage in later literature must determine whether a given word has undergone a change of meaning. Accordingly, the patristic usage of the "Greek fathers" of the early church may teach us whether or not any term of the New Testament employed by them has, by virtue of religious association, departed from its original classical import. They would

know from their religious training whether any word of their vernacular had undergone such change.

GENERIC LAWS.

14. There are two fundamental laws of interpretation which are here called "generic" because of their relation to certain subordinate and subsidiary rules to be stated and illustrated hereafter. If the title, "fundamental laws" should be preferred by any one, he may consider himself at liberty to follow his own inclination or taste in this matter of names. The Hermeneutical principles embodied in these laws are of such primary importance as to constitute the basis of all correct exegesis. The first is the *Law of Harmony, which, as presupposing the unity of truth, requires such interpretation and application of a given passage as is consistent with other undoubted Scripture teaching.* The Saviour himself enforced by his own example the propriety of this law. When at the time of the temptation Satan saw that Jesus repelled his first suggestion by quoting the Scripture, whose teaching was thus honored, the tempter sought to justify his second suggestion by quoting Scripture on his side. The purport of this cunning device was that Jesus should manifest his trust in God and in his divine promise by casting himself over a precipice, since he had Scriptural assurance of being borne up by angelic hands so as to experience no injury. How now was this perversion of Scripture met by our Saviour? He replies: "*It is written again,* Thou shall not tempt the Lord thy God." He thus enforces the idea that no interpretation and application of Scripture can be regarded as admissible that plainly conflicts with divine teaching in other places. It is obvious therefore that the law of harmony underlies all justifiable exposition.

15. The second of the two great principles to which reference is made above we will call *the Law of Opposition, or Negation,* which may be formulated as follows : *In all cases a writer or speaker is liable to suffer injustice, if his statements are interpreted without reference to the contrast before his own mind.* What an author would regard as the precise opposite of any important assertion of truth made by him is *always*, by way of negation, the exact measure of the length and breadth of the signification of that assertion. Hence, any interpreter who would take the assertion out of this relation of opposition and place it in a contrast of his own construction would of necessity do the author injustice.

Here indeed is the underlying source of nearly all incorrect interpretation. When Paul said before the Jewish Sanhedrim, Acts xxiii. 6, "Brethren, I am a Pharisee, the son of a Pharisee," he spoke with reference to the doctrinal issue between the Pharisees and the Sadducees both of which parties were represented in the council. Touching their points of difference he was at that time, as he always had been, on the side of the Pharisees. Now as the Pharisees are described in Paul's own epistles as self-righteous legalists depending on human merit, what kind of interpretation would that be which would represent the apostle as repudiating in his statement before the Sanhedriin his great doctrine of salvation through the grace of God in Christ? It would furnish indeed, a true specimen of a vast amount of exegesis to be found in sermons and religious books. He proclaimed himself a Pharisee only as to the doctrinal difference between the Pharisees and Sadducees.

HERMENEUTICAL RULES.

16. (1). *Interpret every expression in the light of the context, or connection with contiguous statements.* Any exposition given without regard to the context is necessarily unsafe : any exposition given in direct conflict with the context is necessarily false. In recognizing the connection in thought, the unity of truth in a context, this rule is subsidiary to the great "Law of Harmony." And where the context shows a contrast before the mind of the author the rule is also subsidiary to the "Law of Opposition." Jesus in giving instruction to his disciples and enjoining an important duty, Matt. v. 48, speaks as follows : "ye therefore shall be perfect, as your heavenly Father is perfect." It has been supposed that the Master here holds up an absolute standard of perfection in character and requires his followers to constantly strive to reach it, knowing that in this life they could never fully do so. And the last clause, indeed, seems to justify this exposition, namely, the expression, "*as your heavenly Father is perfect.*" This interpretation, nevertheless, is certainly inconsistent with the context which clearly explains the last clause as well as the nature and limited range of the perfection required. The word "therefore" logically connects the passage with the foregoing instruction and shows that the required duty had already been described in the context. Jesus was not discoursing about Christian character in general, but the kind of love that his disciples must manifest

as extending even to enemies and standing thus in contrast with
that of the publicans who loved only those who loved them.
The children of the heavenly Father are expected to be in the
amplitude of their love like him who "makes his sun to rise on
the evil and on the good, and sends rain on the just and on the
unjust." Such imitation of the Father by the children in not
restricting kindness and blessing to friends is described as perfection in love, as contrasted with the meager love in the heart of
the publicans. Hence the requirement: "*Ye therefore shall be
perfect, as your heavenly Father is perfect.*" The term "perfect"
is therefore used relatively.

17. (2). *Interpret in the light of all that is presented in other
passages having any bearing on the matter in hand.* Scriptures
that stand in this relation to one another are commonly called,
"parallel passages." It is obvious that two or more passages
cannot be regarded as subject to the application of this rule unless
they are *really* "parallel." In most cases, indeed, this can be
determined by simple inspection, but there are some instances in
which a careful scrutinizing of the context of each passage is
requisite. When, in II. Cor. v. 7, Paul says: "we walk by
faith, not by sight," he is commonly understood as substantially
saying what he states, in II. Cor. iv. 18; "We look not at the
things which are seen, but at the things which are not seen:
for the things which are seen are temporal; but the things which are
not seen are eternal." Yet the two passages are not parallel, the
contrast presented in the one being widely different from that
brought to view in the other. In II. Cor. iv. 18, the sight referred to is of things "temporal" and the contrasted implied faith
through which believers, look "at the things which are not seen" is
the higher principle of action. In II. Cor. v. 7, the "sight"
referred to is of the heavenly to be hereafter enjoyed and the "faith"
of the contrast is the lower principle of action. Observe the
way the passage reads: "Whilst we are at home in the body, we
are absent from the Lord (for we walk by faith, not by sight);"
we are willing "rather to be absent from the body, and to be present
with the Lord."

18. But the interpreter may not only err in treating as parallel passages that are only apparently so: he may so deal with

those that are really parallel as to obscure the fulness and clear ness of their combined teaching and even to bring them into virtual conflict. The following rule is requisite to make the use of parallel Scriptures subsidiary to the fundamental "Law of Harmony." (3). *Through the suggestive power of words, as indicated by a Verbal Canon above given, a condensed form of expression of necessity implies all that is expressly stated in more elaborate representations of the same matter.* The axiomatic character of this rule, whose importance could scarcely be exaggerated, is recognized by common sense the moment it is formulated. Its essentiality to sound exegesis is readily perceived. Yet no Hermeneutical principle is more frequently or more flagrantly disregarded in interpetàtion. To offset a passage which obviously conflicts with a cherished theory by citing another that may plausibly be construed for the support of that theory is not only to set at naught the harmony of the Scriptures but to proceed in exposition simply under the influence of dogmatic prepossession. To be governed by the axiom above presented will preclude this. When God says to his people through his prophet : "Hear, and your soul shall live," shall we understand that hearing the divine voice, according to the restricted sense ordinarily expressed by that term, is the sole condition of spiritual life? Should we not rather correct such mistake under the application of the rule before us by turning to Jas. i. 22-25. "But be you doers of the word, and not hearers only, deluding your own selves. * * * He that looks into the perfect law, the law of liberty, and so continues, being not a hearer that forgets, but a doer that works, this man shall be blessed in his doing." See also the context of the passage itself. "Incline your ear, and come unto me ; hear, and your soul shall live." All that is expressed in the more elaborate statement, "Incline your ear, and come unto me," is tersely condensed in the one word "hear," and enforced as conditional to the life of the soul.

19. (4). *No interpretation of a passage can be accepted that is manifestly inconsistent with the known purpose of the author, whether regard be had to the general design of the treatise as a whole, or to the special design of the section or paragraph to which the passage belongs.* In some cases the purpose of the writer is declared, as in Jno. xx. 30, 31 ; but in most instances it is to be discovered by a careful reading of the whole treatise with a thoughtful comparison of its several parts with one another. As

John tells us that the object of his record of the supernatural works of Jesus was to produce faith in him as the predicted Messiah, which implies that such was also the object of the other three "Gospels," any interpretation of passages in these books which would explain the miraculous as having simply a benevolent end in view and thus seek to justify the expectation of miracles now, cannot be regarded as legitimate. As a thoughtful perusal of Romans shows the main object of the Epistle to be the demonstration of the freeness and universality of God's grace in the offer of mercy to mankind without respect of persons, that exposition of certain passages in the ninth chapter or other parts of the Epistle which would limit the saving purpose of God to a part of the human race to the exclusion of the remainder involves an inconsistency in the inspired author that effectually disproves the interpretation. In its bearings on the special design of particular sections or paragraphs the rule here under consideration is subsidiary to the great "Law of Opposition." For when a writer is combating some radical error, like a delusive reliance on supposed meritorious claims, it is a manifest injustice to his teaching to overlook his true design and so take his expressions out of the contrast before his own mind and construe them as directed against something else that the interpreter himself may be opposing. Thus to reject legalism as a ground of divine blessing is not to reject religious activity as a condition of such blessing.

20. (5). *Very often a passage cannot be understood apart from the historical circumstances connected with its composition.* This general description embraces especially the time of the writing; the special surroundings of those addressed; their peculiar sentiments and party affiliations, and the like. What is commonly called, "The Lord's Prayer," Matt. vi. 9-13, which has generally been supposed by the religious world to be a model for Christians in all ages, contains no recognition whatever of the mediation of the Lord Jesus and asks for nothing at all in his name. How can this be explained except by considering the fact that it was taught as appropriate *before* Jesus was exalted to the right hand of God to be "both Lord and Christ" in his mediatorial reign under which the imperative direction now is, "whatsoever ye do, in word or in deed, do all in the name of the Lord Jesus, giving thanks to God the Father through him." So of other instructions

as to religious duties and special conditions of blessing before
the inauguration of the New Economy in Christ.   Touching
other features of the rule before us a single illustration must
suffice.   It is said of the Sadducees, in Acts iv. 2, that they came
upon Peter and John "being sore troubled because they taught the
people, and proclaimed in Jesus the resurrection from the dead."
This can be understood only by remembering that the Sadducees
denied the doctrine of a resurrection and future state of existence.
Only those devoted to such unbelief with partisan zeal could be
"sore troubled" that the glorious hope of immortality is made good
for mankind by the triumph of Christ Jesus over death and the
grave.   "Sore troubled" that a new and unanswerable argument
refutes the doctrine of their party by showing that their own existence was not to end in dust !

21. (6).   *When a writer indicates emphasis upon a word or
thought this emphasis must be recognized to obtain the true and
full significance of the passage.*   In the original, emphasis is frequently marked by placing the emphasized word at the beginning
of a statement.   Thus Paul, in I. Cor. iii. 9, rebukes the exaltation of the ministerial instruments of the divine will to the position
of lordship or headship in the church by his emphasis upon the
word "God" to show the sovereign relation which God alone sus-
tains to the church.   In Green's translation the passage reads as
follows : " *God's* work-fellows we are : *God's* husbandry you are,
God's building."   Emphasis here has argumentative force evincing
the thought that Paul, Apollos and others were *but "ministers
through whom"* the Corinthians had believed, and *not lords in whom*
they had believed.   Sometimes emphasis is indicated by contrast, as
when a less important thing is seemingly denied or forbidden to
enhance the superiority of something enforced as infinitely higher.
Thus Jesus, in John vi. 27, says : "Work not for the meat which
perishes, but for the meat which abides unto eternal life."   See
another instance, in I. Pet. iii. 3, 4.

SPECIAL HERMENEUTICAL PRINCIPLES.

22.   The laws of interpretation which have now been set
forth are of universal application.   They must regulate the course
of an interpreter whatever may be the nature of the composition
on which he is at work, whether it be literal or figurative, prosaic
or poetic, historic or prophetic.   But there are certain peculiarities

in figurative language which require the application of special laws, and so also as regards Hebrew poetry and prophetic
diction.

A. Interpretation of Figures.

(A). Definitions.

23. Before submitting any rules in the case it seems proper
to define figurative language and to point out the principal figures
of speech that are found in the Scriptures. A figure of speech
is the extension of a word or expression beyond its ordinary
acceptation for the sake of ornament or force. But there is always
an underlying relation of some sort as the ground of this ornament
or verbal force by which the figurative usage is justified. The
kind of relation in any given case is discernible in the kind of
figure employed. Thus we have the following figures.

(1). *Metaphor;* a figure which applies the name of one
thing to another because of some resemblance, real or supposed,
between them. "Ye are a *temple* of God."

(2). *Simile;* a figure which indicates resemblance by a formal comparison using for this purpose such terms as like, as, etc.
"All flesh is as grass, and all the glory thereof as the flower of
grass."

(3). *Allegory;* a figure which is also based on resemblance,
and indirectly suggests one thing through the representation of
another. In Ps. lxxx. 8-14, Israel is allegorically represented by
a vine. Parables and fables are allegorical representations.
Dr. Carson has clearly shown that allegory is not "metaphor
continued" as some rhetoricians have held. He distinguishes
them as follows. "(*a*). Allegory presents to immediate view the
secondary object only; metaphor always presents the principal
also. (*b*). Metaphor always imagines one thing to be another;
allegory never. (*c*). Every thing asserted in the allegory applies
to the secondary object; every thing asserted in the metaphor
applies to the principal. (*d*). In the metaphor there is but one
meaning; in the allegory there are two, a literal and a figurative.
(*e*). Allegory is a veil; metaphor is a perspective glass.
The former always in some respects conceals the principal
object."

(4). *Metonymy* is a figure which exchanges the name of
one thing for that of another on account of some relation between
them. The principal varieties of the figure will indicate the

kind of relation in each case. (a). The name of the cause is used when reference is made to the effect. Luke xvi. 29: "They have Moses and the prophets," *i. e., their writings.* (b). The effect is named when the cause is meant. Luke ii. 30: "mine eyes have seen thy salvation," *i. e., have "seen the Lord's Christ," the source of salvation. Cf* verse 26. (c). An abstract term is used to represent a concrete reality. Rom. viii. 10: "The spirit is *life* because of righteousness," *i. e., the spirit is living.* (d). The virtual is represented as the actual. I. Cor. xv. 31 : "I die daily." (e). The name of the container is used to denote the thing contained. I. Cor. xi. 26 : "As often as you" "drink the cup."

(5). *Synecdoche*, as well defined by Dr. Blair, is a figure in which "anything less or anything more is put for the precise object meant." Its principal varieties. (a). The whole is put for a part. Luke ii. 1 : "All the world"=Roman Empire. (b). A part is put for the whole. Acts xxvii. 37 : the word "soul," is used to signify the whole man. (c). The genus is put for species. Mark xvi. 15 : "Creature" or creation=moral and intelligent creature or creation. (d). The species is used to denote the genus. Rom. i. 16 : "Greek"=Gentile. (e). A definite number is used for an indefinite I. Cor. xiv. 19 : "five"=very few ; "ten thousand"=very many.

(6). *Antithesis* is a grouping of opposites in a formal contrast. It may be single, twofold, threefold, etc., according to the number of opposite thoughts on each side of the contrast. In Rom. vi. 23 we have a threefold, or triple antithesis. "The *wages* of *sin* is *death;* but the *free gift* of *God* is eternal *life.*" This form of antithesis is of very frequent occurrence and often aids greatly in interpretation. The use of the antithetical arrangement as a help to interpretation is subsidiary to the great "Law of Opposition."

(7). *Paradox* is a figure in which opposites are seemingly affirmed of one and the same subject. "He that finds his life shall lose it." Matt. x. 39. "When I am weak, then am I strong." II. Cor. xii. 10. The force of the figure is in the *apparent opposition* when there is agreement discoverable by considering the difference of meaning in the terms that are employed. When Paul felt his own weakness as a man he could realize that he was "strong in the Lord, and in the strength of his might."

(8). *Irony* is a figure in which what is meant is the opposite of that which is asserted. "No doubt but ye are the people, and wisdom shall die with you." Job. xii. 2. See also Elijah's ironical ridicule of the prophets of Baal. I. Ki. xviii. 27.

(9). *Allusion* is a figure in which a truth is designated by a sort of indirect ironical application of a name falsely employed by others as descriptive of the subject. I. Cor. i. 21: "It was God's good pleasure through the foolishness of the preaching to save those who believe," *i. e.*, through what the philosophic Greeks regarded as "foolishness." See verse 23.

(10). *Hyperbole* is a manifest and impressive exaggeration for the purpose of expressing the full force and increasing the vividness of the subject presented. "Mine eyes run down with rivers of water." Ps. cxix. 136.

(11). *Climax* is such an arrangement of matter that the thought, in regular gradation, *rises from a lower to a higher, or falls from a higher to a lower*, conception. Climax ascending: "All are yours; and ye are Christ's; and Christ is God's." I. Cor. iii. 23. Climax descending: "God hath set some in the church, first apostles, secondly prophets, thirdly teachers, then miracles, then gifts of healings, helps, governments, divers kinds of tongues." I. Cor. xii. 28.

(12). *Personification* is a figure that clothes inanimate objects with the attributes of things animate. "All the trees of the field shall clap their hands."'Is. lv. 12.

(13). *Paronomasia* is a play upon words, a figure in which a word is repeated with a variation in the sense. "Follow me; and leave the dead to bury their own dead." Matt. viii. 22.

(14). *Interrogation*, as a figure of speech, is the asking of a question not for information but to make a strong affirmation or denial. "Who shall lay anything to the charge of God's elect." Rom. viii. 33.

(15). *Anthropomorphism* is a figure which ascribes human features or elements of the human form to God. "The eyes of the Lord are upon the righteous, and his ears unto their supplication. I. Pet. iii. 12.

(16). *Anthropopathy* is a figure that ascribes human affections to God. "It repented the Lord that he had made man on the earth, and it grieved him at his heart." Gen. vi. 6.

(B). RULES.

24. (1). *The interpreter must carefully distinguish between a figurative word and a figurative thing, not looking for a representative object where a mere figure of speech occurs, and vice versa.* When Paul says of the rock from which the Israelites drank that, "the rock was Christ;" he used no figure of speech but pointed to a representative object as a type of him who is the blessed source of "living water." And when Ananias said to Saul: "Arise, and be baptized, and wash away thy sins, calling on his name," he did employ a figure of speech in his use of the term "wash", but made no reference to baptism as a symbolic ordinance or representative institution, any more than Elisha would have indicated a symbolic institution had he said to Naaman, Go to the Jordan and wash away your leprosy. To use a *figure of speech* is one thing, and to *confer upon some object, or ascribe to it a representative character* is wholly a different thing.

25. (2). *We can regard neither a word nor a thing as figurative unless it would involve an absurdity or unreasonable course to do otherwise.* Fanciful exegesis would soon fill the whole Bible with imaginary tropes and fantastic analogies, if interpreters have no law for legitimate distinction between the literal and the figurative. When Jesus said: "I am the true vine, and my Father is the husbandman," we must understand him to speak figuratively for it would be absurd to take his language as literal. And when in the institution of the commemorative supper he said of the loaf: "This is my body," and of the wine: "This is my blood," while he does not use a *figure of speech*, he confers on *the things* of which he speaks a figurative significance or clothes them with a *representative or symbolic character*. The manifold and very gross absurdities involved in the supposition that he speaks of the loaf as his actual body and of the wine as his actual blood ought to lead all men of sense and reflection to see at once that we have here another illustration of the uniform usage which prevails in describing the relation of symbols to things symbolized, as when Paul says of Sarah and Hagar in describing their typical significance: "These women are two covenants," and of the water-furnishing "rock" in the wilderness: "the rock was Christ."

26. (3). *Figures must not be pressed beyond the point or points of resemblance on which is based the lesson intended.* The parables of our Saviour have especially suffered injustice in this respect at the hands of careless interpreters. The true import of a figure must be gathered from the context and the author's design.

27. (4). *The harmony of a figurative description must be preserved throughout its interpretation.* When Paul says to the Corinthians : Ye are "God's building," and then cautions the ministerial builders of this spiritual house to "take heed" as to the kind of materials used in its erection describing the right sort as "gold, silver, costly stones," and the unsuitable kind as "wood, hay, stuble," it is a manifest disregard of the harmony of the figure, and hence a false interpretation, to represent these materials as different *doctrines* preached by those engaged in building up this *personal* house composed of believers in Christ. The figure is evidently the same as that used by Peter in saying: "Ye also, as living stones, are built up a spiritual house." I. Pet. ii. 5.

B. Interpretation of Hebrew Poetry.

28. The influence of Hebrew modes of thought and expression even upon the literature of the New Testament is seen in the reproduction of the poetic parallelism of the Hebrews, and erroneous exegesis has sometimes resulted from a failure to recognize this literary phenomenon. Bishop Lowth, we believe, was the first to point out this striking characteristic of Hebrew poetry. He distinguished three forms of poetic parallelism and to these a fourth form has been added by Bishop Jebb. Parallelism is such an arrangement of corresponding expressions that there is "a certain equality, resemblance or relationship between the members of each period ; so that in two lines or members of the same period, things shall answer to things, and words to words, as if fitted to each other by a kind of rule or measure." The following are its several forms.

29. (1). *Synonymous Parallelism* is the substantial presentation of the same thought under different forms of expression. "When the Lord brings back the captivity of his people, Then shall Jacob rejoice, and Israel shall be glad." Ps. xiv. 7. "Out of Zion shall go forth the law, and the word of the Lord from Jerusalem." Is. ii. 3. See this form of Hebrew parallelism reflected in one of many examples in the New Testament :

"With the heart man. believes unto righteousness; and with the mouth confession is made unto salvation." Rom. x. 10. Manifestly, in the writer's mind, the passage "unto salvation" through confession is the passage "unto righteousness" through belief, and each of the two parallel expressions implies much more than it asserts. Earnest faith in the heart puts one in the way that leads to "righteousness," or "salvation;" and sincere confession of that faith with the mouth commits one to the same way, and so leads on to the same blissful result.

30. (2). *Antithetic Parallelism* is that in which the two members "correspond, one with another, by an opposition of terms and sentiments." Is. i. 19, 20: "If ye be willing and obedient, ye shall eat the good of the land: but if ye refuse and rebel, ye shall be devoured with the sword." This form of parallelism is identical with the figure of antithesis.

31. (3). *Synthetic or Constructive Parallelism* is that in which the correspondence of several parallel members is maintained by a further development in each of the main thought expressed in the first. "The law of the Lord is perfect, restoring the soul: The testimony of the Lord is sure, making wise the simple. The precepts of the Lord are right, rejoicing the heart; the commandment of the Lord is pure, enlightening the eyes. The fear of the Lord is clean, enduring for ever: the judgements of the Lord are true, and righteous altogether." Ps. xix. 7–9. Of this and the two preceding forms of parallelism Bishop Jebb observes that "separately, each kind admits of many subordinate varieties," and that "in combinations of verses, the several kinds are perpetually intermingled; circumstances which at once enliven and beautify the composition, and frequently give peculiar distinctness and precision to the train of thought."

32. (4). *Introverted Parallelism* is that in which the stanzas are so arranged that, whatever may be their number, the first will be parallel with the last, the second with the next to the last, and so on towards the center. The following suffices for illustration:

"My son, if thine heart be wise,
My heart shall be glad, even mine:
Yea, my reins shall rejoice,
When thy lips speak right things."

Prov. xxiii. 15, 16.

C. Interpretation of Prophecy.

33. In speaking of Hermeneutics as a science involving principles which properly applied conduct the interpreter to conclusions which cannot, any more than other scientific results, be accepted on the ground of authoritative decision or dogmatic dictation, exceptional reference was made to a kind of interpretation that does not strictly come within the province of ordinary exegesis. Inspired exposition of typical arrangements, of prophetic symbolism, or of unfulfilled predictions must, of course, be received on the authority of the inspired interpreter; and as with the supernatural *interpretation* of prophecy, so with the superhuman origin of prophecy itself. The power to penetrate the realm of the supernatural rises above the mere application of scientific methods. "No prophecy of Scripture is of private interpretation. For no prophecy ever came by the will of man : but men spake from God, being moved by the Holy Spirit." II. Pet. i. 20, 21. Now to ignore the two limitations here indicated and to use this passage in opposition to the individual right of interpreting the Scriptures in general under the safe guidance of Hermeneutical laws, is to be guilty of dishonest trifling both with the word of God and with the highest interests of mankind. The passage expressly limits what it says to "prophecy of Scripture," and in the reason assigned for the assertion made in the case it still further restricts what it says to the *origin* of prophetic utterance in unfolding that which was previously unknown. It affirms that this supernatural interpretation, or unravelment of divine counsels, was not subject to human option and hence proceeded, not from human foresight, but from the illuminating power of inspiration under which "men spake from God, being moved by the Holy Spirit." But in the context of this passage we learn that we have this "word of prophecy made more sure," or confirmed in the explanatory light of its fulfilment, to which as thus easily understood by ordinary interpretation men may "take heed, *as unto a lamp shining in a dark place.*"

34. (1). Accordingly the first guiding principle, or rule, on this subject may be stated as follows : *The full meaning of prophecy may be found by ordinary intelligence only in the clear light of its undoubted fulfilment.* It required the thrilling scenes of Calvary to explain the fifty-third chapter of Isaiah. Even the prophets themselves "sought and searched diligently" as to the

full import of much that was announced through them by the
Spirit when "it testified beforehand the sufferings of Christ, and
the glories that should follow them."

35. (2). *But in many prophecies there is a blending of type
and antitype indicating a twofold fulfilment, the one temporal
and partial and the other spiritual and complete.* To interpret
predictions without reference to this prophetic feature, as do rationalistic exegetes, is not only to fail to give such explanation as the
terms of many of them demand, but also it is to set aside the authoritative exposition of inspired interpreters. Thus Peter, commenting, in Acts ii. 25-31, on the language employed by David, in Ps.
xvi. 8-10, shows that the expressions used by the psalmist in ref.
erence to himself could only apply to him as the type of Christ
who as "the fruit of his loins" would come forth to fulfil the
prophecy as no other ever had or ever could. David's existing
tomb stood as monumental evidence of the fact that his flesh had
seen corruption and that his soul had not been called from the
spirit land into a reunion with his body and that therefore the
resurrection which he predicted had not been fulfilled in his own
person, but in that of his greater Son, the antitype in prophetic
view. A similar double reference is found in the Saviour's predictions concerning the destruction of Jerusalem, recorded in Mat-
thew xxiv, enabling us to understand what would otherwise remain
inexplicable. In connection with his description of the overthrow
of the doomed city he refers, especially in ver. 29-33, to events
that have not as yet taken place and then, in ver. 34, says : "Verily
I say unto you, This generation shall not pass away, till all these
things be accomplished." In the fearful and tremedous destruction of Jerusalem, many of the Saviour's prophetic expressions
found a literal fulfilment while the rest were typically fulfilled in
this dreadful foreshadowing of the final overthrow of the wicked.

36. (3). Arising from the relation of the prophet to the
matters predicted by him appears another peculiar feature of
prophetic discourse that must be taken into account to understand
correctly much of this kind of Biblical literature. *In a sort of
figurative way the prophet himself is represented as doing that
which results, either directly or indirectly, from his divinely
authorized announcements.* "Go, and tell this people, Hear ye
indeed, but understand not ; and see ye indeed, but perceive not.
Make the heart of this people fat, and make their ears heavy,

and shut their eyes; lest they see with their eyes, and hear with their ears, and understand with their heart, and turn again, and be healed." Is. vi. 9, 10.   Now the Saviour himself in quoting and applying this language has clearly brought out its true meaning.   In Matt. xiii. 14, 15, we read his infallible exposition of the passage : "Unto them is fulfilled the prophecy of Isaiah, which says, by hearing ye shall hear, and shall in no wise understand ; and seeing ye shall see, and shall in no wise perceive : For this people's heart is waxed gross, and their ears are dull of hearing, and their eyes they have closed ; lest haply they should perceive with their eyes, and hear with their ears, and understand with their heart, and should turn again, and I should heal them." Even the event that is directly predicted is ascribed, on the principle under consideration, to the agency of the prophet because of the certainty of its following his unerring announcement.   Hence the form of expression employed by Jehovah in giving Jeremiah his prophetic commission : "See, I have this day set thee over the nations and over the kingdoms, to pluck up and to break down, and to destroy and to overthrow ; to build, and to plant." Jer. i. 10.   This figurative representation of the matter finds its justification in the fact that, since the predicted event, when near at hand, always followed the prophetic announcement before the very eyes of beholders, the prophet himself *seemed* to bring it about.   It was, no doubt, on this account that wicked kings of Israel and of Judah often held the prophets responsible for the state of things that followed and harmonized with their predictions.

THE EXEGETICAL ANALYSIS EXPLAINED.

As prefatory to the analysis of the Epistles presented in the following pages it seems proper to give some explanation of the nature and object of this exegetical process. Expositors are in the habit, to some extent, of dividing the text, as the drift of the sense may indicate, into sections and paragraphs ; but this needful work is not deemed sufficient, and our analysis accordingly is pushed much further and made far more minute. Effort is made to take hold of and exhibit the very fibers of thought that enter into the constitution of each paragraph : to enumerate these ideal elements and express their relation to one another. Suppose a writer makes a statement and then gives a reason and afterwards illustrates either the affirmation or the reason assigned, we will have before us three distinct elements of thought which may be numbered and their connection set forth. Suppose one of these elements has two distinct features, one positive, for example, and the other negative, the analysis may designate these two sub-elements respectively as (A) and (B). Suppose either of these sub-elements should be susceptible of division still more minute, we could indicate this by the letters (a) and (b), etc., as far as the division may extend. And suppose further that an element of thought marked by any of these letters should be substantially repeated by way of explanation or otherwise, this repetition may be indicated by a repetition of the appropriate letter in connection with the figure ². We illustrate from I. Cor. iii. 1 : The religious state of the Corinthians described = "And I, brethren, (A) could not speak unto you as unto spiritual, (B) but as unto carnal, (B²) as unto babes in Christ."

We thus see that among the elements of thought composing a paragraph there are some that are more or less complex and hence in each instance susceptible of analysis into divisions and sub-divisions as far as the nature of the case will admit. And the analysis will disclose the number of elements in every paragraph and their significance in relation to each other. The exegetical student is thus enabled to follow closely the connection and sequence of thought on which a correct interpretation so largely depends, and in this way the exegetical analysis itself, apart from answers to questions at the end of the paragraphs, will furnish the much greater part of the exegesis. It appears

therefore better to undergo this labor than to rest satisfied with
the divisions of sections into paragraphs with notes or answers
to queries appended to each. In the work as printed for the
use of the class room the queries will, in a large measure,
remain unanswered to develop in students, as far as possible,
their capacity to think with the aid of the references given.

Now and then in the analysis an element will present itself
in which the main assertion will be broken by modifying clauses
where transposition will be necessary for the expression of sub-
elements. But this occasional transposition will be the only liberty taken with the text, which will generally be followed as
translated in the Revised Version. Where there are important
deviations from this, the best of all Versions, such departures
will either be vindicated in answers to queries or reference will
be made to some standard author in a foot-note as justifying the
rendering. The aim in this book is, of course, not to undertake
the work of translation but simply that of interpretation. Yet
all who have given sufficient attention to the matter or who have
prosecuted to any considerable extent the labor of an exegete will
indorse the statement that the correct rendering of a passage is
sometimes found to depend, in no little degree, upon the right
interpretation. It would not be difficult to show that erroneous
translations of passages here and there have proceeded from a
failure to apply faithfully to the original the laws of Hermeneutics.

ANALYSIS

OF

FIRST CORINTHIANS.

SECTION FIRST.

THE INTRODUCTION.

i. 1–9.

¶ I. *The Apostolic Greeting. i. 1–3.*

1. The writer officially described=Paul, (A) called to be an apostle of Jesus Christ (B) through the will of God, 1.

2. Designation of his associate=and Sosthenes our brother,

3. Description of those immediately addressed=unto the church of God which is at Corinth, (A) to those who are sanctified in Christ Jesus, (B) called to be saints, 2.

4. Those remotely addressed=with all that call upon the name of our Lord Jesus Christ in every place, their Lord and ours :

5. Benediction=Grace to you and peace (A) from God our Father (B) and the Lord Jesus Christ. 3.

Queries.

(1). What the apostle's idea of a church of Christ, as seen from its two characteristics, in element 3 ; ver. 2? See also I. Pet. ii. 5.

(2). What is it to be "sanctified in Christ Jesus"? 2. Among the Jews whatever was set apart to God was sanctified, and in the higher spiritual setting apart in Christ the cleansing through his blood is required and in Christian usage this last has become the leading thought. *Cf.* Heb. xiii. 12. The modern conceit of sinless perfection does not enter into Scriptural usage. *Cf.* I. Jno. i. 8. Some, indeed, who are here said to be "sanctified in Christ" were only *spiritual babes. Cf.* iii. 1.

(3). How does Paul's use here of the term "saint" differ from the Romish perversion of the word? 2.

(4). What implied in the extension of the teaching of the Epistle to "all who in every place call upon the name of the Lord Jesus Christ"?

(5). What implied in associating the Son with the Father as the source of grace "and peace"? 3. *Cf.* Jno. xiv. 9–11; Philippians ii. 6.

¶ II. *Expression of Gratitude on Account of the Spiritual Advantages of the Corinthians. i. 4–9.*

1. Thanksgiving=I thank my God always concerning you, 4.

2. Ground and occasion of the gratitude=for the grace of God which was given you in Christ Jesus;

3. This grace specified=that in everything you were enriched in him, (A) in all utterance (B) and all knowledge; 5.

4. Ground of this enrichment=even as the testimony of Christ was confirmed in you : 6.

5. Consequence=(A) so that you come behind in no gift; (B) waiting for the revealing of our Lord Jesus Christ; 7.

6. Encouraging assurance=who shall also confirm you unto the end, 8.

7. Ulterior result=that ye be unreproveable in the day of our Lord Jesus Christ.

8. Ground of this assurance=God is faithful, through whom you were called into the fellowship of his Son Jesus Christ our Lord. 9.

Queries.

(1). What the Scriptural import of the word grace and how used in element 2; ver. 4?

(a). See Eph. ii. 4–7; Tit. iii. 4–7, for its proper meaning. (b). Here, as seen in ver. 4, 5, applied to the effect in believers.

(2). How wait for the revealing, or coming, of the Lord Jesus? 7.

(a). Not necessarily expecting this during their own lifetime as this would conflict with II. Thes. ii. 1–5; II. Pet. iii. 4–10. (b). But ever holding themselves in readiness for that great day, not knowing when it might come. *Cf.* II. Pet. iii. 11–14; Matt. xxiv. 30–42.

(3). What the character of the promise in elements 6, 7 ; ver. 7, 8?

Absolute in form but conditional in *sense*. *Cf.* Ezek. xxxiii. 13–16.

SECTION SECOND.
CONCERNING PARTISAN STRIFE AND ITS CONSEQUENCES
i. 10–iv. 21.

¶ I. *Exhortation to Christian Unity and Reproof of Party Spirit. i. 10–17.*

1. Motive to enforce the exhortation=Now I beseech you, brethren, through the name of our Lord Jesus Christ, 10.

2. Contents of the exhortation=(A) that you all speak the same thing, (B) and that there be no divisions among you ; (B²) but that you be perfected together (a) in the same mind (b) and in the same judgement.

3. Occasion of the exhortation=For it has been signified unto me concerning you, my brethren, by those who are of the household of Chloe, that there are contentions among you. 11.

4. Explanation=Now this I mean, (A) that each one of you says, I am of Paul ; (B) and I of Apollos ; (C) and I of Cephas ; (D) and I of Christ. 12.

5. Folly of this emphatically exposed=(A) Is Christ divided? (B) was Paul crucified for you? (c) or were ye baptized into the name of Paul? 13.

6. Ground of thanksgiving in view of their course=I thank God that I baptized none of you, save Crispus and Gaius ; 14.

7. Explanatory reason=lest any man should say that you were baptized into my name. 15.

8. Parenthetical statement on an appeal to memory=(A) And I baptized also the household of Stephanas : (B) besides, I know not whether I baptized any other. 16.

9. The fact of his baptizing but few accounted for=For Christ sent me (A) not to baptize, (B) but to preach the gospel : 17.

Queries.

(1). Why exhort to unity through the name of Christ? 10.

Consult verse 12 and consider the relation of this name to spiritual oneness.

(2). How possible to "be perfected together in the same mind and in the same judgement"? 10.

Notice what is condemned and apply the "Law of Opposition."

(3). Why include among the partisans those who claimed to be "of Christ"? 12.

(4). State the logical force of the questions "was Paul crucified for you?" and "were ye baptized into the name of Paul?"

(5). What bearing has Paul's lack of memory here, ver. 16, upon the question of his inspiration? 16.

Consult Jno. xiv. 26 as to *when* the memory of apostles would be touched by the Spirit. It was not necessary that they should be inspired except as to matters that vitally concerned their *teaching.*

(6). How not sent to baptize? and how did baptism stand related to his commission?

As one sent "to preach the gospel" he was to preach baptism among other duties required by the gospel, but not specially to administer it with his own hands.   And he rejoiced that providentially this important work was mainly committed to others lest the Corinthians should seem to have some apology for their improper use of his name.   "It is evident," says Alford, "that this is said in no derogation of baptism, for he did on occasion baptize–and it would be impossible that he should speak lightly of the ordinance to which he appeals (Rom. vi. 3.) as the seal of our union with Christ."   The context, indeed, clearly shows that Paul is not aiming to disparage baptism, but to rebuke the Corinthians for exalting human names to the position of that divine name which in the great commission stands connected with this ordinance.   "Were ye baptized into the name of Paul"?   Wear that name alone into which you were baptized (Matt. xxviii. 19.) and thus be undivided in recognizing the lordship of Jesus alone.

(7). What bearing has the teaching of this paragraph on the now existing denominationalism?

¶ II.. *The Doctrine of the Cross and Its True Mode of Presentation as Opposed to Partisan Tendencies i. 17–31.*

1. Concluding element of last paragraph as transitional to this=Christ sent me (A) not to baptize, (B) but to preach the gospel: 17.

2. The manner required=not in wisdom of words,

3. Explanatory reason=lest the cross of Christ should be made void.

4. The correct presentation justified by the nature of the gospel=(A) For the doctrine of the cross is to those who are perishing foolishness; (B) but unto us who are being saved it is the power of God. 18.

5. Scriptural anticipation of its effect=For it is written, (A) I will destroy the wisdom of the wise, (B) and the prudence of the prudent will I reject. 19.

6. Evidence of the fulfilment of this prediction=(A) Where is the wise? (a) where is the scribe? (b) where is the disputer of this world? (B) has not God made foolish the wisdom of the world? 20.

7. Occasion and manner of this fulfilment=For seeing that in the wisdom of God (A) the world through its wisdom knew not God, (B) it was God's good pleasure through the foolishness of the preaching to save those who believe. 21.

8. This failure of the world to know God in its own way practically evinced=(A) Seeing that Jews ask for signs, (B) and Greeks seek after wisdom: 22.

9. Their consequent rejection of the divine way=but we preach Christ crucified, (A) unto Jews a stumblingblock, (B) and unto the Gentiles foolishness; 23.

10. The effect different when their own methods are abandoned=but unto those who are called, both Jews and Greeks, (A) Christ the power of God, (B) and the wisdom of God. 24.

11. Ground of this result=Because (A) the foolishness of God is wiser than men; (B) and the weakness of God is stronger than men. 25.

12. Practical illustrative proof on the negative side=For behold your calling, brethren, how that not many wise after the flesh, not many mighty, not many noble, are called: 26.

13. Continued on the positive side=(A) but (a) God chose the foolish things of the world, (b) that he might put to shame those that are wise; (B) and (a) God chose the weak things of

the world, (b) that he might put to shame the things that are
strong; (c) and the lowly things of the world, and the things
that are despised, did God choose, (a) yea and the things that
are not, (b) that he might bring to nought the things that are :
27, 28.

14.   The negative result thus gained=that no flesh should
glory before God. 29.

15.   Underlying ground as seen in God's relation to us=But
of him are you in Christ Jesus, 30.

16.   And brought out more clearly in Christ's relation to us
=who was made unto us (A) wisdom from God, (B) and righteousness (c) and sanctification, (D) and redemption :

17.   Positive result=that, according as it is written, He
that glories, let him glory in the Lord. 31.

Queries.

(1).   How the cross of Christ "made void" by the wisdom
of words? 17.

(a).   It would lay a human rather than a divine basis of
faith. ii. 4, 5.   (b).   It would fail to crucify the flesh which it
does when rightly presented. Gal. vi. 14.

(2).   Account for the expression "the foolishness of the
preaching." 21. Cf. 23.

(3).   What the "doctrine of the cross"? * 18.

(a).   As described in 23, 24, it is that in the preaching
of the cross or death of Christ which was "a stumblingblock" to
Jews and "foolishness" to Greeks, but to believers, the saving
wisdom and power of God in Christ.   (b). As more fully described
in 30 it is that wherein Christ is "made unto us wisdom from
God, and righteousness and sanctification, and redemption."   (c).
A chief element of this "doctrine of the cross" is emphasized by
Peter when he says: (I. Pet. ii. 24) that Christ "bear our sins
in his body upon the tree," identifying this with Isaiah's prophetic
evangelism that "with his stripes we are healed."   This same
"doctrine of the cross" is as offensive to rationalists in our time
as it was in the days of Paul.

---

* Logos staurou=staurology=Cross-doctrine: the religious meaning of the cross and not simply the story of the
crucifixion. Hence, Alford's rendering, "doctrine of the cross" is preferable to that of the Revised Version, "word of
the cross."

¶ III. *Exemplification of These Principles in the Apostle's Preaching at Corinth. ii. 1–5.*

1. Description of his manner of preaching:=And I, brethren, when I came unto you, came not with excellency of speech or of wisdom, proclaiming to you the mystery of God. 1.

2. This required by the nature of his theme=For I determined (A) not to know anything among you, (B) save Jesus Christ, and him crucified. 2.

3. Disclaims anything as due to his own efficiency=And I was with you (A) in weakness, (B) and in fear, (C) and in much trembling. 3.

4. Fuller description of his manner of preaching=And my speech and my preaching (A) were not in persuasive words of wisdom, (B) but in demonstration of the Spirit and of power : 4.

5. End in view=that your faith should not stand (A) in the wisdom of men, (B) but in the power of God. 5.

Queries.

(1). Why speak of the testimony concerning Christ as "the mystery of God"? 1. *Cf.* 7–12.

(2). When Paul asserts that in his preaching he knew only Jesus Christ, why add ; *"and him crucified"*? 2.

See above on "the doctrine of the cross." To Paul, evidently, Christ was no Christ at all apart from his death.

(3). What, according to the context, is *excluded*, and how much is *included*, in limiting preaching to "Jesus Christ, and him crucified"?

All that is foreign to the gospel like the philosophic wisdom of the Greeks, is certainly excluded. But the idea that Christ himself may be placed in contrast with any element of his own teaching, or any requirements of his gospel never entered into the mind of Paul.

(4). How the apostle in weakness, and in fear while at Corinth? *Cf.* Acts xviii. 9, 10.

(5). How was his preaching "in demonstration of the spirit and of power"? 4.

Note the antithesis which will preclude limitation to miraculous manifestations.

¶ IV.   *Concerning the Wisdom of God and the
Method of Its Impartation.   ii. 6–16.*

1. A claim to higher wisdom asserted==Howbeit we speak
wisdom among the perfect : 6.

2. This wisdom negatively described==yet a wisdom (A)
not of this world, (B) nor of the rulers of this world, which are
coming to nought :

3. Positively described==(A) but we speak God's wisdom
(a) in a mystery, (a²) even the wisdom that has been hidden,
(B) which God foreordained before the worlds unto our glory :
(B²) which none of the rulers of this world knows : 7, 8.

4. Proof of their ignorance in the case==for had they known
it, they would not have crucified the Lord of glory : 8.

5. Scriptural evidence that this divine wisdom was utterly
unknown==(A) but [we speak] as it is written, (B) [speaking]
things (a) which eye saw not, (b) and ear heard not, (c) and
which entered not into the heart of man, (a b c) Whatsoever
things God prepared for those who love him. 9.

6. The divine method of making them known==But unto
us God revealed them through the Spirit : 10.

7. Ground of the Spirit's agency in the case==(A) for the
Spirit searches all things, (B) yea, the depths of God. *

8. Simile illustrating the unique relation of the Spirit to
these things==(A) For who among men knows the things of a
man, save the spirit of the man, which is in him? (B) even so the
things of God none knows, save the Spirit of God. 11.

9. Consequent need of apostolic enduement with spiritual
power==(A) But we received, (a) not the spirit of the world,
(b) but the spirit which is of God ; (B) that we might know the
things that are freely given to us by God. 12.

10. The next step in this process of communication described
==Which things also we speak, (A) not in words taught by man's
wisdom, (B) but in words taught by the Holy Spirit ; (B²) com-
bining spiritual things with spiritual. 13.

11. Though thus brought to all, this divine wisdom is still
unknown to some==Now the natural man receives not the things
of the Spirit of God : 14.

---

* "Depths of God" is Green's rendering and brings out the force and beauty of the passage. As the depths of the
sea must be explored to bring forth the hidden treasures, so with the depths of God.

12.   Explanatory reason=for they are foolishness unto him ; 14.

13.   The underlying cause=(A) and he cannot know them, (B) because they are spiritually judged.

14.   The high plane of the spiritual man in contrast=(A) But he that is spiritual judges all things, (B) and he himself is judged of no man [that is not spiritual]. 15.

15.   Evidence of this=(A) For who (a) has known the mind of the Lord, (b) that he should instruct him? (B) But we have the mind of Christ. 16.

Queries.

(1).   Who "the perfect" that are capable of understanding the divine wisdom? ver. 6. *Cf.* iii. 1.

(2).   Show from ver. 7–11 that the term "mystery" in Scriptural usage denotes the undiscoverable, rather than the incomprehensible, matters of revelation as distinguished from that which may be known through philosophy or science.

(3).   How the spiritual things spoken "in words taught by the Holy Spirit"? 13.

(a).   Not that the Spirit dropped, as it were, every word into the minds of the apostles, for this would be irreconcilable with differences of style on their part. (b).   But, as the context shows, the Spirit so guarded the faculty of expression as to preclude the use of unsuitable terms, just as it influenced the memory only when it became necessary.

(4).   Who "the natural man" that regarded the divine wisdom as "foolishness"? 14. *Cf.* i. 23.

(5).   Show that the spiritual man is not the converted man as distinguished from the unconverted—not the regenerate *as such.* 15. *Cf.* iii. 1.

(6).   Explain, accordingly, the incapacity both of the natural man (i. 14) and of the "babes in Christ" (iii. 1) for judging spiritual things.

(a).   The former by using a false standard of measurement, philosophic wisdom, rejected the only means of spiritual enlightenment.   (b).   The latter, though accepting the true means, had made only a beginning of Christian development. The full grown or spiritually enlightened stands in contrast with both. Hence the incapacity for properly judging of spiritual things was due to lack of training (ver. 2, 3) not to any native or constitutional defect.

¶ V. *Reproof of the Corinthians for Lack of Spiritual Wisdom as Evinced by Their Carnal Divisions. iii. 1–4.*

1. Description of their religious state=And I, brethren, could not speak unto you (A) as unto spiritual, (B) but as unto carnal, (B²) as unto babes in Christ. 1.

2. The teaching adapted to this infantile condition=(A) I fed you with milk, (B) not with meat; 2.

3. Explanatory reason=(A) for ye were not able to bear it : (B) nay, not even now are you able; (B²) for ye are yet carnal : 2, 3.

4. Proof of this=for whereas (A) there is among you jealousy and strife, (B) are ye not carnal, (B²) and walk after the manner of men? 3.

5. More specific statement of this proof=For are ye not men? (A) When one says, I am of Paul; (B) and another, I am of Apollos; 4.

Queries.

(1). How "babes in Christ," *i. e., regenerate persons*, said to be "carnal"? 1.

Apply here the third "Verbal Canon" and "Law of Opposition."

(2). How carnal "babes" to become spiritual men? *Cf.* I. Pet. ii. 2.

(3). What light does the inability of these "carnal" persons to receive higher spiritual birth throw on ii. 14?

¶ VI. *Proper Estimate of Ministers as Determined by Their Work. iii. 5–15.*

1. Office of Paul and Apollos=(A) What then is Apollos? (B) and what is Paul? (A B) Ministers through whom ye believed ; 5.

2. True source of their ministerial efficiency=and each as the Lord gave to him.

3. Their work metaphorically described=(A) I planted, (B) Apollos watered ; 6.

4. Result due to divine agency alone=but God gave the increase.

5. Logical conclusion=(A) So then neither is he that plants anything, (A²) neither he that waters; (B) but God that gives the increase. 7.

6. Equality of ministers with only a difference of labour and reward=(A) Now he that plants and he that waters are one: (B) but each shall receive his own reward according to his own labour. 8.

7. Their subordination to God in their ministerial equality =God's co-workers [with each other] we are: 9.

8. Consequent assertion of the divine sovereignty over the Corinthian church=(A) God's husbandry ye are, (B) God's building.

9. Metaphorical description of his own work at Corinth= I laid a foundation; (A) according to the grace of God which was given unto me, (B) as a wise masterbuilder 10.

10. The work of others who came after him=and another builds thereon.

11. A caution to these=But let each man take heed how he builds thereon.

12. Reason for not extending this caution to the work of laying the foundation=(A) For other foundation can no man lay than that which is laid, (B) which is Jesus Christ. 11.

13. Ground of the caution just given=But if any man builds on the foundation gold, silver, costly stones, wood, hay, stubble; (A) each man's work shall be made manifest: (B) for the day shall declare it, (B²) because it is revealed in fire; (A²) and the fire itself shall prove each man's work of what sort it is. 12, 13.

14. Statement of consequences=(A) If any man's work shall abide which he built thereon, he shall receive a reward. (B) If any man's work shall be burned, he shall suffer loss: 14, 15.

15. The result as to the builder=but he himself shall be saved; 15.

16. Condition of this result=yet so as through fire.

Queries.

(1). Through what instrumentality came the faith and consequently the salvation of the Corinthians? Cf. 5; i. 21.

(2). While being thus honored as instruments in the work of salvation how can it be said that neither is he that plants nor he who waters anything? 7.

It is not they in any measure, but God altogether who gives the increase. Apply Law of Opposition.

(3). Vindicate against Alford and others the view given in the analysis of the "fellow-workers" mentioned in ver. 9.

To suppose that it is "contrary to usage" to represent here the planter (Paul) and the waterer (Apollos) as co-workers with each other under God as his servants in this fellowship of service is to beg the question and that too in the face of two very clear proofs to the contrary supplied by the passage itself and its context. (a). The emphasis in the original is upon the word God three times used and placed each time at the beginning of a clause : " *God's* fellow-workers we are : *God's* husbandry you are; *God's* building." The construction is exceptional in placing the genitive in the first place with strong emphasis and there is no usage elsewhere similar to it. Paul had said that "he who plants and he who waters are one" as co-workers in the fellowship of the same service. Well, whose laborers are they as thus co-working with each other? The answer emphatically is " *God's.*" (b). The whole context shows that Paul is here exposing the overestimate of ministers by the Corinthians in virtually elevating them above the sphere of minister or servant to that of Lord. "Neither is he who plants anything, neither he who waters ; but God who gives the increase." To represent them therefore *in this connection* as "fellow-workers with God" would be utterly foreign to the drift of thought and rather confirmatory of the Corinthian idea.

(4). As the building here referred to is personal (ver. 9 and 16) what are the materials that enter into it?

It is strange that Commentators in general represent these as "various matters of doctrine" proclaimed by the ministerial builders. Meyer, for example, after presenting this view says : "Our exposition is, in fact, a *necessity*, because it alone keeps the whole figure in harmony with itself throughout. For if the *foundation* which is laid be the contents of the first preaching of the gospel, namely *Christ*, then the *material wherewith the building is carried on* must be the contents of *the further instruction given.*" This exposition, instead of being a "necessity" by preserving "the whole figure in harmony with itself throughout" is, in fact, an

absurdity through the *destruction* of that very harmony.   If, as
Meyer admits, "the building is the *church*, ver. 9, which is being
built * * * the church as a building with a personal foundation,
and consisting of persons" how can doctrines rather than persons
be regarded as the materials that enter into this building?   And as
Christ is confessedly, "a personal foundation," it cannot be instruction concerning Christ that constitutes this foundation, nor "the
further instruction given" that constitutes the material of the
building.   The simple conception is that Christ is presented not as a
doctrine but as a person, and believers are represented as being
brought through a personal faith into personal relations with Christ
himself ; and this is the building of which the apostle speaks.

(5).   How are these materials to be tested by fire and how
classified with reference to this test? 13.

We need not suppose any reference to the fire of the final
judgement as do expositors in general ; for whether the work of
each builder will prove to be genuine and so abide as incombustible
gold, silver and costly stones, in the presence of fire ; or worthless,
as combustible wood, hay and stubble will be determined by a
fire in this world. *Cf.* I. Pet. iv. 12; i. 6, 7.

(6).   How the builder suffer loss, if his work is burned?
Examine the antithesis.   Suffer the loss of his reward.

(7).   How will the builder himself be saved as through fire? 15.
If he comes out of it as gold and does not perish as stubble or
hay.

(8).   How can worthless material as wood, hay and stubble
be said to be built upon Christ? 12-14.

Just as the dead branch is mechanically connected with the
true vine. Jno. xv. 2.

¶ VII.   *Indication of the Source of the Pernicious Tendencies
at Corinth and Admonitions Respecting the Same.   iii. 16-23.*

1.   The sacredness of God's people intimated=Know ye not
(A) that ye are a temple of God, (B) and that the Spirit of God
dwells in you? 16.

2.   A warning indicative of this sacredness=If any man
destroy the temple of God, him shall God destroy ; 17.

3.   Explanatory ground of this warning=(A) for the temple
of God is holy, (B) which temple ye are.

4.   Admonition touching the true source of this mischief=
Let no man deceive himself.   (A) If any man thinks that he is

wise among you in this world, (B) let him become a fool, that he may become wise. 18.

5. The admonition justified=For the wisdom of this world is foolishness with God. 19.

6. Scriptural evidence of this statement=(A) For it is written, He that takes the wise in their own craftiness : (Job v. 13) (B) and again, The Lord knows the reasonings of the wise, that they are vain. 19, 20; Ps. xciv. 11.

7. Hortatóry conclusion=Wherefore let no one glory in men. 21.

8. Explanatory reason=For all things are yours; (A) whether Paul, (B) or Apollos, (C) or Cephas, (D) or the world, (E) or life, (F) or death, (G) or things present, (H) or things to come; 21, 22.

9. Reason expanded into climax=(A) all are yours; (B) and ye are Christ's; (C) and Christ is God's. 22, 23.

Queries.

(1). What, according to the context, is the difference between the use of the word "*temple*," in ver. 16, and its use in vi. 19?

(2). How is one to "become a fool that he may become wise"? ver. 18, 19. *Cf.* ii. 6.

¶ VIII. *Corollary of the Foregoing Discussion Setting Forth the True View of Ministerial Worth and Responsibility. iv. 1-5.*

1. Correct estimate of himself and his co-workers=Let a man so account of us, (A) as of ministers of Christ, (B) and stewards of the mysteries of God. 1.

2. Chief requisite in the case=Here, moreover, it is required in stewards, that a man be found faithful. 2.

3. This test not subjected to human judgement=But with me it is a very small thing (A) that I should be judged of you, (B) or of man's judgement : (B²) yea, I judge not mine own self. 3.

4. Reason for regarding such judgement as inapplicable= For I know nothing against myself; (A) yet am I not hereby justified : (B) but he that judges me is the Lord. 4.

5. Consequent admonition=Wherefore judge nothing before the time, until the Lord come, 5.

6. Ground of his just judgement in the case=who will (A) both bring to light the hidden things of darkness, (B) and make manifest the counsels of the hearts;

7. Final result=and then shall each man have his praise from God.

Queries.

(1). What the nature of the faithfulness demanded of the Lord's ministerial "stewards"? 2.

(a). In the light of II. Tim. ii. 2 as compared with I. Tim. iv. 16, among other passages, it may be seen that nothing short of an unswerving adherence to the simple gospel of Christ is divinely regarded as filling the required measure of this faithfulness. (b). And from this it is clear that a false religious liberalism that would tamper with the affairs of God is paralleled only by the "unrighteous steward" of Luke xvi. 1–12 who was *very liberal* with the property of another!

(2). How "judge nothing"· "until the Lord shall come"?

5. Here apply the Law of Opposition.

¶ IX. *Reasons for Lowliness Enforced by a Contrast between the Assumed Self-sufficiency of the Corinthians and the Real Condition of the Apostles. iv. 6–13.*

1. Mode of handling his theme=Now these things, brethren, I have in a figure transferred to myself and Apollos for your sakes; 6.

2. His object in this=that in us you might learn not to go beyond the things which are written;

3. Ulterior end=that no one of you be puffed up for the one against the other.

4. Argument against this partisan emulation=(A) For who makes thee to differ? (A²) and what hast thou that thou didst not receive? (B) but (a) if thou didst receive it, (b) why dost thou glory as if thou hadst not received it? 7.

5. Derision of their self-sufficiency by an ironical climax= (A) Already are you filled, (B) already you are become rich, (C) you have reigned without us: 8.

6. Serious wish parenthetically inserted=(A) yea .and I would that you did reign, (B) that we also might reign with you.

7. Reason for this in continued parenthesis=For, I think, (A) God has set forth us the apostles last of all, as men doomed to death : (B) for we are made a spectacle unto the world, (a) even to angels, (b) and to men. 9.

8. Ironical derision resumed=(A) We are fools for Christ's sake, but you are wise in Christ; (B) we are weak, but you are strong; (C) you have glory, but we have dishonour. 10.

9. The last thought expanded in a literal description=Even unto this present hour (A) we both hunger, and thirst, (B) and are naked, (C) and are buffeted, (D) and have no certain dwellingplace; (E) and we toil, working with our own hands : 11, 12.

10. Description of their deportment under this treatment =(A) being reviled, we bless; (B) being persecuted, we endure; (C) being defamed, we intreat.: 12, 13.

11. This picture of apostolic suffering for others completed in climax=(A) we are made as the filth of the world, (B) the offscouring of all things, even until now. 13.

Queries.

(1). Was the transfer of the matters here considered a transfer to Paul and Apollos as only *some* of those concerned or a transfer of that to them which wholly pertained to others? 6. *Cf.* i. 14-17.

(2). How "not to go beyond what is written" in our esteem for men? 6. *Cf.* i. 31.

(3). Explain the argument in element 4; ver. 7, against partisan emulation.

Granting the excellency that was claimed whence was it derived? Glory in nothing borrowed.

¶ X. *The Apostle's Explanation of the Character and Spirit of His Reproofs and Admonitions. iv. 14-21.*

1. His purpose in what he had written=(A) I write not these things to shame you, (B) but to admonish you as my beloved children. 14.

2. Justification of this parental mode of address=(A) For though you should have ten thousand tutors in Christ, (B) yet have ye not many fathers : (B²) for in Christ Jesus I begat you through the gospel. 15.

3. Exhortation based on this, his relation to them=I beseech you therefore, be ye imitators of me. 16.

4. Reference to a paternal effort as already made to secure this end=For this cause have I sent unto you Timothy, (A) who is my beloved and faithful child in the Lord, (B) who shall put you in remembrance of my ways which be in Christ, 17.

5. More specific indication of the "ways" referred to=even as I teach everywhere in every church.

6. A false view of Timothy's mission alluded to=Now some are puffed up, as though I were not coming to you. 18.

7. Avowal of his purpose in opposition to this=But I will come to you shortly, if the Lord will; 19.

8. Predicted result=and I will know, (A) not the word of those who are puffed up, (B) but the power.

9. Ground of this procedure=For the kingdom of God (A) is not in word, (B) but in power. 20.

10. Alternative as to the manner of his coming submitted= What will you? (A) shall I come unto you with a rod, (B) or in love (B²) and a spirit of meekness? 21.

Queries.

(1). Comparing iv. 15 with iii. 5 what do we learn as to the spiritual results of Paul's ministry, and what light is thus thrown on the subject of spiritual influence?

(2). What special propriety in the reference in this connection to Timothy as the apostle's son in the faith? 17.

A father sends one child to other children (ver. 15) in thoughtful manifestation of parental tenderness.

SECTION THIRD.
CONCERNING LICENTIOUSNESS.
v. 1–vi. 20.

¶ I. *Censure of the Deliberate Toleration of a Gross Case of Incest. v. 1-8.*

1. Ground of complaint==It is actually reported (A) that there is fornication among you, (B) and such fornication as is not even among the Gentiles, (B²) that one of you has his father's wife. 1.

2. Their state of mind in the presence of this sin==(A) And

you are puffed up, (B) and did not rather mourn, that he who
had done this deed might be taken away from among you. 2.

3.   The apostle's position in reference to this matter=For
I verily, being absent in body but present in spirit, have already,
as though I were present, judged him that has so wrought this
thing, 3.

4.   Consequent decision in the case=in the name of our
Lord Jesus, you being gathered together, and my spirit, with the
power of our Lord Jesus, to deliver such a one unto Satan 4, 5.

5.   Object of this=(A) for the destruction of the flesh, (B)
that the spirit may be saved in the day of the Lord Jesus. 5.

6.   Contrast between their supposed excellency and their
real condition as resulting from this sin=(A) Your glorying is
not good. (B) Know you not that a little leaven leavens the whole
lump? 6.

7.   Consequent exhortation=(A) Purge out the old leaven,
(B) that you may be a new lump, (B²) even as you are [by pro-
fession] unleavened. 7.

8.   Ground of this exhortation=For our passover also has
been sacrificed, even Christ :

9.   Hortatory conclusion=wherefore let us keep the feast,
(A) not with old leaven, (A²) neither with the leaven of malice
and wickedness, (B) but with the unleavened bread of sincerity
and truth. 8.

Queries.

(1).   Why the allegation in ver. 2 that the Corinthians were
"puffed up"? 2.

Paul had *already*, especially in iv. 6-8, referred to this self-
conceit and supercilious vanity of the Corinthians over their supposed spiritual excellency and Christian wisdom and he now contrasts this imaginary state of excellence with the *real condition of
moral degradation* to which the deliberately tolerated "leaven" of
corruption in their midst was bringing the whole church. To
suppose, as do some, that they were "puffed up" *over the case of
incest itself* is absurd and arises from a careless forgetfulness of
what had been previously written.

(2).   How the apostle's spirit present at Corinth to act with
the church in this case? 4.

Through the instructions which his supernaturally enlightened spirit here gives.

(3). What the deliverance to Satan to which reference is made in 5? Cf. 2, 7, 13,

(4). How for the destruction of the flesh that the spirit may be saved? 5. Cf. Gal. v. 17-21 ; Col. iii. 5, 6.

(5). Explain the allusions in the concluding exhortation. Analogy to Jewish passover.

¶ II. *Correction of Their Misunderstanding of a Commandment Previously Given as to Association with Fornicators.*
v. 9-13.

1. Reference to an injunction formerly given=I wrote unto you in my epistle to have no company with fornicators; 9.

2. Negative explanation=(A) not altogether with the fornicators of this world, (B) or with the covetous and extortioners, (c) or with idolaters; 10.

3. Reason for not including these=for then must you needs go out of the world :

4. Positive explanation=but now I write unto you (A) not to keep company, if any man that is named a brother, (a) be a fornicator, (b) or covetous, (c) or an idolater, (d) or a reviler, (e) or a drunkard, (f) or an extortioner; (B) with such a one no, not to eat. 11.

5. Justification of this limitation=(A) For what have I to do with judging those who are without? (B) Do not you judge those who are within, (A^2) whereas those who are without God judges? 12, 13.

6. Injunction to use in the case of the incestuous man their power of judging those within=Put away the wicked man from among yourselves. 13.

Queries.

(1). What eating not allowed in 11?

No reference here to the Lord's supper, but to a social meal which among the Orientals was the highest expression of social recognition.

(2). Why restrict the prohibition to those within? 12.

From the nature of its object which was the reformation of those for whose conduct the church was responsible.

¶ III. *Digressive Censure of Litigation before Outside Tribunals, Suggested by the Above Mentioned Province of Believers to Judge All Within. vi. 1–11.*

1.   Strong reprobation of lawsuits among brethren=Dare any of you, having a matter against his neighbor, (A) go to law before the unrighteous, (B) and not before the saints? 1.

2.   Argument *a fortiori* evincing the absurdity of. this course =(A) Or know you not that the saints shall judge the world? (B) and if the world is judged by you, are you unworthy to judge the smallest matters? 2.

3.   Second argument *a fortiori*=(A) Know you not that we shall judge angels? (B) how much more, things that pertain to this life? 3.

4.   Consequent injunction=If then you have to judge things pertaining to this life, set those to judge who are of no account in the church. 4.

5.   Their need of this admonition=I say this to move you to shame. 5.

6.   Consequent reproachful inquiry=Is it so, (A) that there cannot be found among you one wise man, (A²) who shall be able to decide between his brethren, (B) but (a) brother goes to law with brother, (b) and that before unbelievers? 5, 6.

7.   Emphatic censure of their course=Nay, already it is altogether a defect in you, that you have lawsuits one with another. 7.

8.   Suggestion of a preferable course=(A) Why not rather take wrong? (B) why not rather be defrauded?

9.   Their course the very reverse of this=Nay, but (A) you yourselves do wrong, and defraud, (B) and that your brethren. 8.

10.   Consequent interrogative warning=Or know you not that the unrighteous shall not inherit the kingdom of God? 9.

11.   The warning repeated and emphasized by a detailed specification=(A) Be not deceived : (B) there shall inherit the kingdom of God. (a) Neither fornicators, (b) nor idolaters, (c) nor adulterers, (d) nor effeminate, (e) nor abusers of themselves with men, (f) nor thieves, (g) nor covetous, (h) nor drunkards, (i) nor revilers, (j) nor extortioners, 9, 10.

12.   The former relation of Corinthian believers to these characters=And such were some of you : 11.

13. Their present condition in contrast=(A) but you were washed, (B) but you were sanctified, (C) but you were justified

14. The sphere within which these results are effected=(A) in the name of the Lord Jesus Christ, (B) and in the Spirit of our God.

Queries.

(1). How the saints to judge the world? 2. *Cf.* Rev. iii. 21.

(2). How shall we judge angels? 3. Connect Jude 6 with the last reference.

(3). Why follow the marginal reading of the Revised Version in verse 4?

Because the reading as pointed in the text of this Version would imply that the Corinthians were setting some incompetent persons in the church to judge in the case and are here reproved for so doing. But the fact is they were going outside of the church entirely for judges and Paul's relative injunction in the matter is that it would be better to take the least suitable in the church to act as judges than to go outside. The next verse shows that he would, of course, have them to select *wise* and suitable brethren to judge in the case.

(4). What the underlying ground for the prohibition of litigation among Christians? *Cf.* Jno. xviii. 36.

(5). Set forth the different phases of salvation presented in element 13; ver. 11.

"Washed"=cleansed through pardon. *Cf.* Acts xxii. 16: "sanctified"=set apart to God through this cleansing. *Cf.* Heb. xiii. 12; also ix. 14: "justified"=accepted of God as righteous through this same cleansing. Rom. iv. 6–8.

(6). How all this effected "in the name of the Lord Jesus Christ, and in the Spirit of our God"?

"The sense is," says Canon Evans, "you were baptized, you were consecrated, you were justified all in the hallowed circle of his redemptive name, and in the pure and light-shedding sphere of the Spirit of God." *Cf.* Matt. xxviii. 19.

❡ IV. *Remonstrance against Confounding Gentile Libertin-
ism with Christian Liberty. vi. 12–20.*

1. Assertion of liberty in things indifferent with the first
limitation=(A) All things are lawful for me;(B) but not all
things are expedient. 12.

2. Assertion of liberty with the second limitation=(A) All
things are lawful for me; (B)but I will not be brought under the
power of any.

3. Illustration=(A) Meats for the belly, (B) and the belly
for meats : 13.

4. Transitory character of this relation=but God shall bring
to nought both it and them.

5. Wide difference from this in the relations of the body
asserted=(A) But the body is not for fornication, (B) but for
the Lord; (B²) and the Lord for the body :

6. Permanency of this relation=(A) and God both raised
the Lord, (B) and will raise up us through his power. 14.

7. Its consequent sacredness emphasized=Know you not
that your bodies are members of Christ? (A) shall I then take
away the members of Christ, (B) and make them members of a
harlot? (B²) God forbid. 15.

8. The great contrast of results adduced as an argument=
(A) Or know you not that he that is joined to a harlot is one
body? (A²) for, The twain, says he shall become one flesh. (B)
But he that is joined unto the Lord is one spirit. 16, 17.

9. Consequent positive warning=Flee fornication. 18.

10. Additional argument to deter them based on the heinous character of this sin=(A) Every sin that a man does is with
out the body; (B) but he that commits fornication sins against
his own body.

11. Final ground of prohibition=Or know you not (A) that
your body is a temple of the Holy Spirit (a) which is in you, (b)
which you have from God? (B) and you are not your own; 19.

12. Proof of a divine ownership=for you were brought with
a price : 20.

13. Consequent exhortation=glorify God therefore in your
body.

Queries.

(1). How other sins without the body and this against the
body? ver. 18. *Cf.* ver. 16.

(2). How the citation of verse 16 a proof that "he who is joined to a harlot is one body" with her? 16.

(3). What implied in element 6; verses 13, 14, as to the nature of the resurrection? See also xv. 44.

SECTION FOURTH.

Concerning Marriage. vii. 1–40.

¶ I. *Rights and Obligations of Married Life. vii. 1–7.*

1. Reply to a previous inquiry from Corinth=Now concerning the things whereof you wrote : It is good for a man not to touch a woman. 1.

2. Limitation of this general affirmation=But, because of fornications, (A) let each man have his own wife, (B) and let each woman have her own husband. 2.

3. Obligation in each case=(A) Let the husband render unto the wife her due : (B) and likewise also the wife unto the husband. 3.

4. Ground of this obligation=(A) The wife (a) has not power over her own body, (b) but the husband : (B) and likewise also the husband (a) has not power over his own body, (b) but the wife. 4.

5. Consequent direction as to the use of this conjugal right =Defraud you not one the other, (A) except it be by consent for a season, (B) that you may give yourselves unto prayer, (A²) and may be together again, 5.

6. Evil result to be thus avoided=that Satan tempt you not because of your incontinency.

7. Character of this instruction=But this I say (A) by way of permission, (B) not of commandment. 6.

8. Underlying reason for giving, in this case, counsel and not requirement=(A) Yet I would that all men were even as I myself. (B) Howbeit each man has his own gift from God, (a) one after this manner, (b) and another after that. 7.

Queries.

(1). How "defraud ye not one the other, except it be by consent," etc.? 5.

Neither party to wedlock to deprive the other of the conjugal "due" (1, 2) except within the limitations prescribed.

(2). How this instruction given "by way of permission, not of commandment"? 6.

As will be clearly seen further on, the apostle under inspiration permits or advises, rather than commands, the persons here addressed to waive for a season their right in view of certain advantages. The idea that Paul himself was permitted to give some religious instruction simply on his own individual judgement apart from spiritual illumination is utterly foreign to the context. No apostle ever dared to advance mere opinions in acting as a religious teacher.

¶ II. *Inspired Counsel for the Unmarried and Imperative Injunctions for the Married. vii. 8-16.*

1. Instruction for the unmarried=But I say to the unmarried and to widows, (A) It is good for them if they abide even as I. (B) But if they have not continency, let them marry : (B²) for it is better to marry than to burn. 8, 9.

2. Difference in the *character* and *form* of instruction for the married=But unto the married (A) I give charge, (B) yea (a) not I, (b) but the Lord, 10.

3. The instruction in the case=(A) That the wife depart not from her husband (B) (but and if she depart, (a) let her remain unmarried, (b) or else be reconciled to her husband) ; 10, 11.

4. The instruction for the husband identical=and that the husband leave not his wife.

5. The *form* of instruction for those married to unbelievers =But to the rest (A) say I, (B) not the Lord : 12.

6. The duty imposed in the case=(A) If any brother has an unbelieving wife, (a) and she is content to dwell with him, (b) let him not leave her. (B) And the woman who has an unbelieving husband, (a) and he is content to dwell with her, (b) let her not leave her husband. 13.

7. Explanatory reason=(A) For the unbelieving husband is sanctified in the wife, (B) and the unbelieving wife is sanctified in the brother : 14.

8. Proof of this from a case analogous=(A) else were your children unclean ; (B) but now are they holy.

9. Duty when the unbelieving is unwilling to dwell with the other consort=Yet if the unbelieving depart, let him depart : 15.

10. Ground of this instruction=(A) the brother or the sister is not under bondage in such cases : (B) but God has called us in peace.

11. Ulterior reason for this instruction=(A) For how knowest thou, O wife, whether thou shalt save thy husband? (B) or how knowest thou, O husband, whether thou shalt save thy wife? 16.

Queries.

(1). Why does the apostle wish others to abide in single life even as did he? 8. See 26.

(2). How does the instruction given in ver. 10 differ as to *character* from that given in vers. 6–8; and how does it differ in *form* from that given in ver. 12?

In ver. 10 he gives inspired *commandment* which cannot be disregarded without sin, whereas he had previously given inspired *advice*, which, though infallible as to the best course to pursue under the circumstances might, nevertheless, for sufficient reason, not be followed, yet be attended with all the inconvenient consequences. *Cf.* 28. As to *form*, this instruction differs from that given in ver. 12, in that it is based on an utterance of the Saviour himself, *cf.* Mark x. 11, 12, whereas, that in ver. 12, comes only through Paul as his inspired apostle.

(3). How the unbelieving sanctified in the believing husband or wife? 14.

The word sanctified, in this place, is employed according to the broader sense of the word in Jewish usage. Compare, as similar to this, the use of the equivalent word "*cleansed*," in Acts x. 15 and 28.

(4). How their children said to be "holy"? 14.

This use of the word "holy" is analogous to that of the term "sanctified," as above. "Paul proves," says Meyer, "that the non-believing husband is sanctified through his believing wife; for just as in the children's case, that which makes them holy is simply the specific bond of union with Christians (their parents) ; so, too, in the case of the mixed marriage, the same bond of union must have the same influence. Had the baptism of Christian children been then in existence Paul could not have drawn this inference, because in that case the holiness of such children would have had *another* basis."

(5). How the brother or sister "not under bondage" when the unbelieving husband or wife departs? 15.

He does not mean that the person is released from wedlock, for if the departing remarries he sins on the ground that she is still his wife ; the instruction therefore, is restricted by what is said in 11.

¶ III. *The General Principles Set Forth in the Instruction Above Given Applied to Other Civil Relations. vii. 17–24.*

1. A General direction=Only, so let him walk. (A) As the Lord has distributed to each man, (B) as God has called each, 17.

2. Its universality of application=And so ordain I in all the churches.

3. Illustration=(A) Was any man called (a) being circumcised? (b) let him not become uncircumcised. (B) Has any been called (a) in uncircumcision? (b) let him not be circumcised. 18.

4. Ground of this instruction=(A) Circumcision is nothing, (A²) and uncircumcision is nothing; (B) but the keeping of the commandments of God. 19.

5. Substantial repetition of the general injunction=Let each man abide in that calling wherein he was called. 20.

6. Second illustrative example=(A) Wast thou called (a) being a bondservant? (b) care not for it: (B) but (a) if thou canst become free, (b) use it rather. 21.

7. Reason for this indifference to temporal bondage=(A) For he that was called in the Lord, (a) being a bondservant, (b) is the Lord's freedman: (B) likewise he that was called, (a) being free, (b) is Christ's bondservant. 22.

8. Ground of this, their relation, to Christ=Ye were bought with a price; 23.

9. Consequent injunction=become not bondservants of men.

10. Concluding reproduction of the first general direction= Brethren, let each man, wherein he was called, therein abide with God. 24.

Queries.

(1). As directed in ver. 21 "use" what rather than what?

It is strange that many able exegetes should regard this as an exhortation to continue in the bondage to which reference is made, rather than accept the liberty offered. They seek to justify this on grammatical and contextual grounds. Besides the absurdity of supposing that a deliberate choice of bondage is enforced where a state of freedom is providentially offered, this construction represents the apostle as teaching the Corinthians to be resigned to the divine will in accepting with contentment a lot in life and at the same time refusing to follow the leadings of the divine will in providentially offering a better condition. Neither the context nor any manipulation of the particles here employed can be forced to justify such an absurdity. Surely, the requisition to be content with any lot in life, when it seems to be the divine will that such a lot should continue, is perfectly harmonious with the willingness to accept an improved condition when the same divine will seems to indicate it. Yet Alford, for example, speaks of the "utter inconsistency" of the one with the other, and Meyer supposes that for Paul thus to teach would "be contravening his own thrice-repeated injunction : let each remain," etc. As to the particles used in the original, a simple literal rendering of them, in the order of their occurrence, harmonizes with the interpretation presented above. After enjoining contentment, where one is involved in a state of bondage, the apostle adds "but if also thou art able to become free, use it (*i. e.*, this ability or providential opportunity,) rather." In other words, besides enjoining resignation to the divine will in a given case, he also teaches the acceptance of the divine favor which would providentially lead to a higher condition.

(2). How "become not bondservants of men"? ver. 23.

Here applied spiritually according to the antithesis presented. Recognize no lordship in men where Christ Jesus alone should reign over the soul. This teaching condemns the blind and slavish subjection to a priesthood whose members while pretending to represent the Lord Jesus, slyly substitute their own will for his. The Corinthians had seen something of this spirit. *Cf.* II. Cor. xi. 20.

¶ IV. *Inspired Advice to the Unmarried in View of Circumstances Then in Existence. vii. 25–35.*

1. Character and form of instruction to the unmarried= Now concerning virgins (A) I have no commandment of the Lord : (B) but I give my judgement, (B²) as one that has obtained mercy of the Lord to be faithful. 25.

2. His counsel in the case=I think therefore that this is good by reason of the present distress, namely, that it is good for a man to be as he is. 26.

3. Application=(A) Art thou (a) bound unto a wife? (b) seek not to be loosed. (B) Art thou (a) loosed from a wife? (b) seek not a wife. 27.

4. Evidence that this instruction for the unmarried is simply advisory=(A) But and if thou marry, thou hast not sinned; (B) and if a virgin marry, she has not sinned. 28

5. His discouragement of marriage under the circumstances sufficiently justified by its consequences=(A) Yet such shall have tribulation in the flesh : (B) and I would spare you [this tribulation].

6. Additional justification=But this I say, brethren, the time is shortened, (A) that henceforth both those that have wives may be as though they had none; (B) and those that weep, as though they wept not; (C) and those that rejoice, as though they rejoiced not; (D) and those that buy, as though they possessed not : (E) and those that use the world, as not using it to the full : 29, 30, 31.

7. Explanatory reason=for the fashion of this world passes away. 31.

8. Third ground of his advice=But I would have you to be free from cares. 32.

9. Illustration=(A) He that is unmarried is careful for the things of the Lord, (A²) how he may please the Lord : (B) but he that is married is careful for the things of the world, (B²) how he may please his wife. 32, 33.

10. Ground on which this is equally applicable to Christian women=And there is a difference also between the wife and the virgin. 34.

11. Illustration=(A) She that is unmarried is careful for the things of the Lord, (A²) that she may be holy (a) both in body (b) and in spirit : (B) but she that is married is careful for the things of the world, (B²) how she may please her husband.

12. His object in giving this advice=And this I say for your own profit; (A) not that I may cast a snare upon you, (B) but for that which is seemly, (B²) and that you may attend upon the Lord without distraction. 35.

Queries.

(1). Show that the apostle's "judgement" or decision, ver. 25, is not a mere expression of his own private opinion as a man. 25.

(a). The contrast here is as before, ver. 10, between instruction through Paul and the oral teaching of Christ; difference of <u>form</u>, not a difference as to <u>authority</u>. The instruction

also takes the *character* of *advice*, not that of imperative obligation involved in commandment. (b). That it proceeded from
the inspiring Spirit and not from Paul's own wisdom is clear
from the fact that he gives it as "one that has obtained mercy of
the Lord to be *faithful*," which implies close adherence to divine
teaching. *Cf.* iv. 1, 2. (c). In closing these instructions in ver.
40 the apostle himself distinctly, though in a modest way, claims
as their true source the Spirit's illumination.

(2). What the "present distress" in view of which the
apostle gives this advice? 26.

(3). Import of the expression : "the time is shortened."
Cf. as similar. xv. 31.

(4). How the unmarried woman *holy* both in body and
spirit? 34.

¶ V. *Instructions for Fathers as to the Marriage of Their
Daughters under the Circumstances in View. vii. 36–38.*
    1. When a father should consent to the marriage of a daughter
=(A) let him do what he will; (A²) he sins not; (B) let them
marry. (a) But if any man thinks that [by refusing] he behaves
himself unseemly toward his virgin daughter, (b) if she be past
the flower of her age, (c) and if need so requires, 36.
    2. When he may withhold his consent=But he shall do well.
To keep his own virgin daughter [from marriage], (A) that stands
steadfast in his own heart, (B) having no necessity, (B²) but has
power as touching his own will, (C) and has determined this in
his own heart, 37.
    3. The conclusion=So then (A) both he that gives his own
virgin daughter in marriage does well; (B) and he that gives her
not in marriage shall do better. 38.
¶ VI. *Instruction as to the Marriage of Widows. vii. 39, 40.*
    1. Instruction touching a second marriage=A wife (A) is
bound for so long time as her husband lives; (B) but if the husband be dead, she is free to be married to whom she will; 39.
    2. The limitation advised=only in the Lord.
    3. Recommendation of a preferable course=But she is hap-
pier if she abide as she is, after my judgement : 40.

4.   Ground of this "judgement," or advice=and I think that I also have the Spirit of God.

SECTION FIFTH.
RELATION OF LIBERTY TO SELF-DENIAL.
viii. 1–xi. 1.

¶ I.   *Christian Liberty as Related to the Eating of Meats Offered to Idols. viii. 1–13.*

1.   General introductory statement=Now concerning things sacrificed to idols : We know that we all have knowledge. 1.

2.   Parenthetical contrast between pride of knowledge and helpful love=(A) Knowledge puffs up, (B) but love builds up.

3.   This contrast extended=(A) If any man thinks that he knows anything, he knows not yet as he ought to know ; (B) but if any man loves God, the same is known of him. 2, 3.

4.   Return to the general statement=Concerning therefore the eating of things sacrificed to idols, (A) we know that no idol is anything in the world, (B) and that there is no God but one. 4.

5.   Explanatory justification of this statement=(A) For though there be that are called gods, (a) whether in heaven (b) or on earth ; (A²) as there are gods many, and lords many ; (B) yet to us there is one God, the Father, (a) of whom are all things, (b) and we unto him ; (B²) and one Lord, Jesus Christ, (a) through whom are all things, (b) and we through him. 5, 6.

6.   Evidence of the insufficiency of this to determine one's action in relation to others=Howbeit in all men there is not that knowledge : (A) but some, (a) being used until now to the idol, (b) eat as of a thing sacrificed to an idol ; (B) and their conscience being weak is defiled. 7.

7.   Reason for abstaining for the sake of such from the eating of sacrificial meat=But meat will not commend us to God : (A) neither, if we eat not, are we the worse ; (B) nor, if we eat, are we the better. 8.

8.   Caution as to the use of the liberty claimed in the matter=But take heed lest by any means this liberty of yours become a stumblingblock to the weak. 9.

9.   Ground and necessity for this admonition=For if a man see thee who has knowledge sitting at meat in an idol's temple, (A) will not his conscience, if he is weak, be emboldened to eat

things sacrificed to idols? (в) For through thy knowledge he that is weak perishes, (в²) the brother for whose sake Christ died. 10, 11.

10. The heinous character of thus leading one into moral conflict with himself=(ᴀ) And thus, sinning against the brethren, and wounding their conscience when it is weak, (в) you sin against Christ. 12.

11. Emphatic conclusion=Wherefore, if meat makes my brother to stumble, (ᴀ) I will eat no flesh for evermore, (в) that I make not my brother to stumble. 13.

Queries.

(1). How far does Paul in this paragraph deal with the question touching the relation of Christian liberty to the eating of things sacrificed to idols?

Only so far as to decide that whatever privilege a believer may have, or may even think that he has in the case, he cannot exercise it apart from the practical manifestation of Christian love and so in a way that would be detrimental to others. Hence, the somewhat abrupt contrast at the very beginning of the discussion between inflation through the conceit of knowledge and spiritual upbuilding through the power of love. The Corinthians, it seems, had asked the apostle whether a Christian could innocently eat meats of offerings that had been made to heathen idols. It is clear from his treatment of the matter in this section, partly in the eighth chapter and partly in the tenth, that he could not give to this question as a whole either an affirmative or a negative answer ; but proceeds, as we shall see in due time, to draw a distinction in the case that is *universally* overlooked. For the present he apparently concedes what he afterwards emphatically prohibits, because his present purpose is to enforce the sacred demands of Christian love.

(2). What measure of "knowledge" does Paul undoubtedly concede as possessed by those who claimed the "liberty" to which reference is made in ver. 9, 10? *Cf.* ver. 4–6.

(3). What two false inferences did they draw from this "knowledge" giving clear proof of the fact that each one at that time knew "not yet as he ought to know"?

(a). They erroneously supposed that since "no idol is anything in the world," no reality whatever stood as the object of idolatrous offerings. (b). They thence still further erroneously concluded that they could go with impunity into an idol's temple and sit at meat at an idol's table. *Cf.* x. 19–22.

(4). Guided then by the fixed and imperative law that requires the interpretation of a passage in the clear light of other Scriptures bearing on the subject, how are we to understand the expression ; "this liberty of yours" in ver. 9?

As signifying simply, "this liberty" that you claim, but which in practical exercise will lead one into unconscious "communion with demons" according to the decision in x. 19–22.

(5). In view of all this, how is the believer who *rightly* denied this claim of "liberty" represented as a "weak" brother?

(a). *Certainly not* because of any unreasonable prejudice in the case or false and narrow conception of a privilege allowed by the gospel of Christ, since the supposed "liberty" that he opposes is decided by Paul to be no liberty at all, but a pernicious practice. (b). But it is seen, by comparing ver. 7 with ver. 10, that the weakness to which reference is made is of a far more dangerous character. It is located in the *moral realm* and consists in a *weakly yielding* to the influence of another's example *against one's own convictions of right* and thus resulting in internal moral conflict and wounding of conscience. Thousands with very little knowledge have been morally strong enough to stand by their convictions amid the flames, while many highly enlightened persons have weakly denied their faith in the face of danger.

(6). This being undeniable, how does the apostle associate in ver. 7 this moral weakness with lack of knowledge as to divine unity and the nothingness of idols? 7.

The connection here is incidental. The mental confusion of some as to the divine unity and the nature of idols to which reference is made by the apostle presented the occasion of divergence among the Corinthians as to the *practical question* indicated in ver. 10. With this difference the danger of manifesting moral weakness became possible if the objector to the practice should be led by the influence of others to disregard his convictions of right. And if he yielded to that influence against the protest of his conscience, he would show moral weakness whatever might be his reasons for supposing the practice to be wrong : whether he thought, incorrectly, that a sort of deity actually existed as the object of the offering, or rightly believed that no deity but a demon existed in the case. Had he known perfectly that the things offered in heathen worship are not offered to a deity but to a demon and with this knowledge had eaten at the idol's table the sacrificial meat as a *thing offered to a demon* and thus against his convictions of right, his weakness would have been *precisely the same.* Thus there is no essential connection between lack of knowledge and the dangerous weakness to which the apostle refers.

(7). Explain Paul's conception of Christian liberty in relation to self-denial as shown by his own example. *Cf.* ver. 13; ix. 19–22; x. 32, 33.

¶ II. *The Apostle's Statement of the Rights and Privileges Which He Had Waived in the Interest of Others. ix. 1–14.*

1. His claim and rank=(A) Am I not free? (B) am I not an apostle? 1.

2. Proof of this=(A) have I not seen Jesus Christ our Lord? (B) are not you my work in the Lord?

3. The logical force of this=(A) If to others I am not an apostle, (B) yet at least I am to you: (B²) for the seal of mine apostleship are you in the Lord. 2.

4. Response to such as would dispute his claim=My defence to those who examine me is this. (A) Have we no right to eat and to drink? (B) Have we no right to lead about a wife that is a believer, 3, 4, 5.

5. Precedent for the exercise of this right=(A) even as the rest of the apostles, (B) and the brethren of the Lord, (C) and Cephas? 5.

6. Assertion of this privilege as equally applicable to himself and Barnabas=Or I only and Barnabas, have we not a right to forbear working? 6.

7. Argument by analogy in favor of his claim=(A) What soldier ever serves at his own charges? (B) who plants a vineyard, and eats not the fruit thereof? (C) or who feeds a flock, and eats not of the milk of the flock? 7.

8. A still higher ground of his claim=(A) Do I speak these things after the manner of men? (B) or says not the law also the same? 8.

9. Scriptural citation in proof of this=For it is written in the law of Moses, Thou shalt not muzzle the ox when he treads out the corn. 9.

10. Indication of a typical reference in this legal provision =(A) Is it for the oxen that God cares, (B) or says he it altogether for our sake? 9, 10.

11. Application of the typical meaning=Yea, for our sake it was written : (A) because he that plows ought to plow in hope, (B) and he that threshes, to thresh in hope of partaking. 10.

12. This agricultural illustration extended to an argument *a fortiori*=(A) If we sowed unto you spiritual things, (B) is it a great matter if we shall reap your carnal things? 11.

13. Second argument *a fortiori* based on their accordance of these rights to others= (A) If others partake of this right over you, (B) do not we yet more? 12.

14. Reference to his self-denial in the case=Nevertheless (A) we did not use this right ; (B) but we bear all things,

15. Ground of this course=that we may cause no hindrance to the gospel of Christ.

16. Final argument based on the divine provision for the support of the Old Testament ministry=(A) Know you not that they who minister about sacred things eat of the things of the temple, (B) and they who wait upon the altar have their portion with the altar? 13.

17. Logical conclusion=Even so did the Lord ordain that they who proclaim the gospel should live of the gospel. 14.

Queries.

(1). What connection between his apostolic claim and his having seen the Lord? ver. 1. *Cf.* Acts xxvi. 16-18.

(2). How a "yet more" tenable ground than others had he for a right to support by the Corinthians? ver. 12. *Cf.* iv. 15.

¶ III. *The Apostle's Testimony as to His Self-Denial in Relation to These Rights. ix. 15-23.*

1. His course in reference to these privileges=But I have used none of these things : 15.

2. Misapprehension of his defence of his claim obviated= and I write not these things that it may be so done in my case :

3. His reason for this self-denial=for it were good for me rather to die, than that any man should make my glorying void.

4. The ground of this glorying exists elsewhere than in the work of preaching=For if I preach the gospel, I have nothing to

glory of; (A) for necessity is laid upon me; (B) for woe is unto me, if I preach not the gospel. 16.

5. Further explanation=(A) For if I do this of mine own will, I have a reward: (B) but if not of mine own will, I have a stewardship intrusted to me. 17.

6. Indication of his only ground of glorying and inquiry as to his reward in the case=What then is my reward, that I while preaching, render the gospel without cost in order not to use my power in the gospel? * 18.

7. Answer suggesting his reward and bringing it forward as a reason prompting his action=For though I was free from all men, I brought myself under bondage to all, that I might gain the more. 19.

8. This illustrated=(A) And to the Jews (a) I became as a Jew, (b) that I might gain Jews; (A²) to those who are under the law, (a) as under the law, not being myself under the law, (b) that I might gain those who are under the law; (B) to those who are without law, (a) as without law, not being without law to God, but under law to Christ, (b) that I might gain those who are without law. (c) To the weak (a) I became weak, (b) that I might gain the weak: 20, 21, 22.

9. Generalization=(A) I am become all things to all men, (B) that I may by all means save some. 22.

10. Ground of the whole procedure=And I do all things for the gospel's sake, that I may be a joint partaker thereof. 23.

Queries.

(1). Bring out the full meaning of the distinction presented in ver. 17.

From the context and scope of reasoning the apostle evidently means that what he does as a matter of duty imposed, like his work of preaching, involves the idea of a stewardship intrusted to him that *must* be carried out; whereas a mere *voluntary* course such as waiving his right to a support was creditable with some sort of reward.

(2). How can voluntary service more than other service entitle the servant of the Lord to a reward? 17.

Only in the way of grace and not as of a meritorious claim as this would conflict with Rom. iv. 5.

Alford's rendering and punctuation, the correctness of which will be shown in answer to a query.

(3).   How did Paul become "all things to all men"? 22.

(4).   Why, with Alford, place an interrogation point at the end of ver. 18 rather than after the word "reward" near the beginning as in most translations?

The old punctuation represents Paul as stating that the waiving of his right to support in preaching was his reward for waiving that right! The doing of a thing is represented as the reward for doing it! The new punctuation represents the gaining of more for Christ by this course than would otherwise be saved as his regard for adopting this course. This makes good sense while the other representation involves an absurdity.

¶ IV.   *Enforcement of the Duty of Self-denial by Reference to the Grecian Games. ix. 24-27.*

1.   Allusion to the race-course=Know you not that they who run in a race (A) run all, (B) but one receives the prize? 24.

2.   Hortatory application=Even so run, that you may attain.

3.   Self-denial indispensable to success=And every man that strives in the games is temperate in all things. 25.

4.   Infinitely higher reason for its observance in our case= (A) Now they do it to receive a corruptible crown; (B) but we an incorruptible.

5.   Consequent compliance of the apostle himself with this condition of success=(A) I therefore so run, as not uncertainly; (B) so fight I, as not beating the air: (B^2) but (a) I buffet my body, (b) and bring it into bondage: 26, 27.

6.   Reason=lest by any means, (A) after that I have preached to others, (B) I myself should be rejected. 27.

Queries.

(1).   What lesson to be derived from the antithesis of *all* running, and *one* receiving the prize? 24.

(2).   What lesson as to the power of self-control to be learned from those who strive "in the games"? 25.

(3).   What bearing has Paul's reason for earnest self-conflict, ver. 27, on the question touching the possibility and danger of utter apostasy?

¶ V. *Exhortation to Self-denial Based on Typical Elements of Jewish History. x. 1-13.*

1. Israel's spiritual advantages on the exodus from Egypt=
For I would not, brethren, have you ignorant, (A) how that our
fathers were all under the cloud, (B) and all passed through the
sea; (A B) and were all baptized unto Moses in the cloud and in
the sea; (c) and did all eat the same spiritual meat; (D) and did
all drink the same spiritual drink : 1-3, 4.

2. Proof of this spiritual enjoyment=(A) for they drank of
a spiritual rock that followed them : (B) and the rock was Christ.
4.

3. Evidence of a forfeiture of these privileges=(A) Howbeit with most of them God was not well pleased : (B) for they
were overthrown in the wilderness. 5.

4. Typical significance of these events=(A) Now these
things were our examples, (B) to the intent (a) we should not
lust after evil things, (b) as they also lusted. 6.

5. Practical illustration by specification=(A) Neither be
you idolaters, as were some of them ; (A²) as it is written, (a)
The people sat down to eat and drink, (b) and rose up to play.
(B) Neither let us commit fornication, (a) as some of them committed, (b) and fell in one day three and twenty thousand. (c)
Neither let us tempt the Lord, (a) as some of them tempted, (b)
and perished by the serpents. (D) Neither murmur you, (a) as
some of them murmured, (b) and perished by the destroyer. 7-10.

6. The lesson of typical warning re-asserted=(A) Now
these things happened unto them by way of example; (B) and
they were written for our admonition, upon whom the ends of
the ages are come. 11.

7. Consequent exhortation=Wherefore (A) let him who
thinks he stands (B) take heed lest he fall. 12.

8. The possibility of heeding this admonition indicated=
There has no temptation taken you but such as man can bear : 13.

9. Ground of this possibility=but God is faithful, (A) who
will not suffer you to be tempted above that you are able ; (B)
but will with the temptation (a) make also the way of escape,
(b) that you may be able to endure it.

Queries.

(1). How "baptized unto Moses"? 2. Compare the expression "baptized into Christ." Rom. vi. 3 ; Gal. iii. 27.

(2). How baptized "in the cloud and in the sea"? 2.
Cf. Ex. xiv. 21, 22, and note the elements of the description here given by Paul. They were *"in* the sea" and *"under* the cloud," and so *"passed through* the sea." They were thus *enveloped* till they passed from under the cloud and out of the sea. "The cloud" and "the sea," says Bengel, "took the fathers out of sight and restored them again to view, much as water does those who are baptized." The cloud over them was a cloud of protecting glory : hence, they went through "on dry ground" whereas the storm cloud over the Egyptians, described in Ps. lxxvii. 11–2Q and to which reference is made by Josephus, poured its fury upon the latter to their utter destruction.

(3). Who included among the "baptized"?
(a). Regarded as a mere physical envelopment everybody and everything even to the beasts of burden, the carriages and utensils of the Israelites. (b). But Paul by no means presents this typical baptism in any such light. He looks upon it as a *voluntary* and *spiritual* procedure flowing from intelligence and deliberation, as evinced by his use of the middle voice in the original : they "had themselves baptized unto Moses." And its antitype, *Christian baptism*, equally involves moral and spiritual elements, as no mere mechanical and physical act can constitute any part of Christianity or possess any religious value whatever.

(4). The "rock that followed them," How? 4.
Just as the manna followed them. The rock of the desert was ever ready to be stricken as need required and God directed. Hence, more than one smiting of the rock took place showing that the individual rock first smitten did not roll after the Israelites as some have supposed.

(5). How assert that "the rock was Christ"?
See Biblical Hermeneutics : paragraph 24.

(6). Why the term *"all"* five times repeated and emphasized in ver. 1–4, and what bearing has the implied contrast on the question of apostasy?

(7). What the import and warning power of the expression : "Let him who *thinks* he stands take heed lest he fall"? ver. 12.

¶ VI. *The Eating of Sacrificial Meat at an Idol's Table or in Idolatrous Feasts Prohibited. x. 14-22.*

1. Warning suggested by the chief sin of the Israelites above specified=Wherefore, my beloved, flee from idolatry. 14.

2. Appeal to their common sense to decide as to the force of his reasoning=(A) I speak as to wise men ; (B) judge you what I say. 15.

3. First argument to justify the prohibition to follow=(A) The cup of blessing which we bless, is it not a communion of the blood of Christ? (B) The bread which we break, is it not a communion of the body of Christ? 16.

4. Explanation=(A) seeing that we, (a) who are many, (b) are one bread, (b²) one body : (B) for we all partake of the one bread. 17.

5. Second argument=Behold Israel after the flesh : have not they who eat the sacrifices communion with the altar? 18.

6. False inference obviated=What say I then? (A) that a thing sacrificed to idols is anything, (B) or that an idol is anything? 19.

7. True import of the argument brought out=But I say that the things which the Gentiles sacrifice, (A) they sacrifice to demons, (B) and not to God : 20.

8. Consequent prohibition=and I would not that you should have communion with demons.

9. Ground of this prohibition=(A) You cannot drink the cup of the Lord, and the cup of demons : (B) you cannot partake of the table of the Lord, and of the table of demons. 21.

10. Warning against a disregard of the prohibition=(A) Or do we provoke the Lord to jealousy? (B) are we stronger than he? 22.

Queries.

(1). What turn in the discussion is made by this paragraph?

Through the warning allusion to the idolatry of the Israelites the apostle, having enforced the duty of self-denial, returns to the consideration of the question touching the eating of things sacrificed to idols, deals now with this question on its own merits, and advances so far as to forbid absolutely the eating of such meat at an idol's table. ver. 20, 21.

(2). How reconcile this prohibition with viii. 9, 10?

Paul did not in the eighth chapter raise the question as to the propriety of "sitting at meat in an idol's temple" as his purpose then was simply the enforcement of the duty of love through self-denial, and hence he only *apparently* granted as a "liberty" what he now prohibits as sinful. He who boasted of his "knowledge" in the case knew "not yet as he ought to know" touching the nature of his supposed "liberty" which instead of being such would only involve him in unconscious "communion with demons." Yet to decide that those on the other side of this practical issue were right in their denial does not imply that they were fully acquainted with the true ground on which this denial could be justified. We do not therefore read any part of the tenth chapter into the eighth but simply interpret the latter in the light of the former.

¶ VII.   *Christian Liberty as Regards Meats Offered to Idols When Eaten at Private Meals.   x. 23–xi. 1.*

1.   Restriction of liberty=(A) All things are lawful; (B) but all things are not expedient. (A²) All things are lawful; (B²) but all things edify not. 23.

2.   This modification of liberty by expediency explained= (A) Let no man seek his own, (B) but each his neighbor's good. 24.

3.   Liberty conceded in the eating of sacrificial meat sold in the market=(A) Whatever is sold in the shambles, eat, (B) asking no question for conscience sake; 25.

4.   Scriptural ground of this liberty=(A) for the earth is the Lord's, (B) and the fulness thereof. 26. *Cf.* Ps. xxiv. 1.

5.   Application of the modifying principle stated above=(A) If one of those who believe not bid you to a feast, and you are disposed to go; (a) whatsoever is set before you, eat, (b) asking no question for conscience sake. (B) But if any man say unto you, This has been offered in sacrifice, (a) eat not, for his sake that shewed it, (b) and for conscience sake : 27, 28.

6.   This reference to conscience explained=conscience, I say, (A) not thine own, (B) but the other's; 29.

7. Justification of this instruction=(A) for why is my liberty judged by an other conscience? (B) If I by grace partake, why am I eyil spoken of for that for which I give thanks? 30.

8. Hortatory conclusion from this=therefore do all to the glory of God. (A) Whether you eat, (B) or drink, (C) or whatsoever you do, 31.

9. Consequent admonition=Give no occasion of stumbling, (A) either to Jews, (B) or to Greeks, (C) or to the church of God: 32.

10. Consistency of this with his own example=even as I also please all men in all things, (A) not seeking mine own profit, (B) but the profit of many, (B^2) that they may be saved. 33.

11. His example enforced=(A) Be you imitators of me, (B) even as I also am of Christ. xi. 1.

Queries.

(1). How does Paul here apply the principle of expediency?

Rather for the abridgment than enlargement of liberty as circumstances may require.

(2). What liberty is now granted as to the eating of meats sacrificed to idols, and what distinction is here drawn on the subject? *Cf.* 25–27.

The eating of such meat at a private meal as distinguished from the wrongful participation of such in idolatrous feasts at an idol's table.

(3). What duty does the apostle still enforce involving the restriction of this liberty?

The manifestation of Christian love through self-denial according to circumstances. *Cf.* 28–33.

(4). Explain the relation of ver. 29, 30 to the main thought here enforced.

The apostle does not, as a thoughtless reader might suppose, deny the limitation of this liberty through the dictates of another's conscience, but the very reverse, his meaning being, according to the connection, why should I so use my liberty as to call down upon its exercise the judgment of another's conscience?

(5). Show the harmony between the teaching of this paragraph and the decision of the apostles in Acts xv. 29.

The apostle is here carrying out the very meaning and spirit of that decree in forbidding the use of meat offered to idols,

when the peace and fellowship of Christian brethren are broken
up or interrupted by this act. If the Jerusalem decree is regarded
as universally binding for all time, it is irreconcilable with the
liberty granted in ver. 27 of this chapter. To suppose that this
is granted as a liberty only when one is ignorant of its true
nature, involves the idea that one may do what is wrong in itself,
if he will only close his eyes to the true character of his act.
Notice, too, that in prohibiting the eating of such meat at private
meals when some brother present objects, the prohibition is not
based on any alleged wrong in the act itself which should equally
concern the conscience of all, but it is simply "for his sake" who
objects and solely in deference to his conscience. Hence, the
apostle adds : "conscience, I say, not thine own, but the other's."
Moreover, the consideration that Paul in this discussion makes no
reference whatever to the decision at Jerusalem ought to lead us
to conclude that this decision has no bearing on the question which
the apostle now has before him except in so far as the interests of
fellowship are concerned.

(6). Reconcile this teaching of Paul with Rev. ii. 14, 20.

The context of the passages in Revelation and the historical
record to which reference is made alike show that the eating of
sacrificial meat offered to idols there condemned, belonged to the
idolatrous worship that Paul has as strongly condemned in the
foregoing paragraph. *Cf.* his decision in ver. 20–22.

SECTION SIXTH.
CONCERNING DISORDERS IN PUBLIC WORSHIP IN THE
CORINTHIAN CHURCH. xi. 2–34.

¶ I. *Disapproval of the Manner in Which Women Prayed
and Prophesied in Public. xi. 2–16.*

1. Preliminary commendation=Now I praise you (A) that
you remember me in all things, (B) and hold fast the traditions,
(B²) even as I delivered them to you. 2.

2. Doctrinal ground of the ensuing instruction=But I would
have you know, (A) that the head of every man is Christ ; (B) and
the head of the woman is the man ; (c) and the head of Christ is
God. 3.

3. Inference from this=(A) Every man praying or prophesying, having his head covered, dishonours his head. (B) But
every woman praying or prophesying with her head unveiled

dishonours her head : (b²) for it is one and the same thing as if she were shaven. 4, 5.

    4. Argument from this virtual identity stated in full=(a) For if a woman is not veiled, (a²) let her also be shorn : (b) but if it is a shame to a woman to be shorn or shaven, (b²) let her be veiled. 6.

    5. Ground of this difference of position=For a man indeed ought not to have his head veiled, (a) forasmuch as he is the image and glory of God : (b) but the woman is the glory of the man. 7.

    6. Explanatory justification of this statement=(a) For (a) the man is not of the woman ; (b) but the woman of the man : (b) for neither (a) was the man created for the woman ; (b) but the woman for the man : 8, 9.

    7. Conclusion from this=for this cause (a) ought the woman to have a sign of authority on her head, (b) because of the angels. 10.

    8. Harmony of this relative sphere of each with the mutual dependence of both=Howbeit (a) neither is the woman without the man, (b) nor the man without the woman, in the Lord. 11.

    9. Evidence of this=(a) For as the woman is of the man, (b) so is the man also by the woman ; 12.

    10. The whole arrangement divinely ordered=but all things are of God.

    11. Appeal to their own sense of propriety in the case= Judge you in yourselves : is it seemly that a woman pray unto God unveiled? 13.

    12. Natural ground of this appeal=Does not even nature itself teach you, (a) that, if a man have long hair, it is a dishonour to him? (b) But if a woman have long hair, it is a glory to her ; (b²) for her hair is given her for a covering. 14, 15.

    13. Authoritative determination of the question=But if any man seems to be contentious, (a) we have no such custom, (b) neither the churches of God. 16.

Queries.

    (1). What the "traditions" to which reference is made in ver. 2, and how distinguished from the "traditions" condemned by Jesus in Matt. xv. 3–9?

    The sense of Paul's statement will be brought out in greater clearness if in the translation we enable the English reader to see what is apparent to the reader of the original, that the word represented by "traditions" is repeated in the verb form. Paul would thus say : you "hold fast the *deliverances*, even as I *delivered* them to you." He thus refers to the elements of what Jude calls, "the faith which was once for all *delivered* unto the saints" and which we now have embodied in the New Testament. The idea that there were to be certain instructions for religious guidance existing apart from the apostolic writings and handed down from generation to generation, thus becoming "traditions," as the word is now often used, is utterly foreign to the thought of the apostle. *Inspired deliverance* from the tongue or pen of an apostle of Jesus Christ *is one thing*, and the changeful transmission from age to age of teaching claiming to be of God but absolutely unknown to the Holy Scriptures, *is an entirely different* thing. It suits the interests and the purposes of Rome to confound the two, and of her in reference to her traditions it may truly be said, as did Jesus of the Pharisees concerning their traditions : you make "void the word of God because of your tradition. * * * In vain do they worship me teaching as their doctrines the precepts of men."

(2). What "head" dishonoured when a man with covered head, or a woman with uncovered head, prophesies or prays? Ver. 4, 5. *Cf.* ver. 3.

(3). What the *probable* meaning of the reference to the angels in ver. 10? *Cf.* Is. vi. 2.

(4). How does *nature* teach that long hair is a glory to a woman and a dishonour to a man? 14.

¶ II. *Reproof of the Corinthians on Account of Their Gross Perversion of the Lord's Supper.* *xi. 17–34.*

1. Limitation of the praise which he had bestowed=But in giving you this charge, I praise you not, (A) that ye come together not for the better (B) but for the worse. 17.

2. Explanatory reason=For first of all, when ye come together in the church, (A) I hear that divisions exist among you ; (B) and I partly believe it. 18.

3. Inference as to the result==(A) For there must also be heresies among you, (B) that they which are approved may be made manifest among you. 19.

4. This course subversive of their object in assembling==When therefore ye assemble yourselves together, it is not possible to eat the Lord's supper : 20.

5. Explanatory reason=for in your eating (A) each one takes before other his own supper; (B) and one is hungry, (C) and another is drunken. 21.

6. Argument against this perversion of the Lord's supper into a carnal feast=What? (A) have ye not houses to eat and to drink in? (B) or despise ye the church of God, (C) and put those to shame who have not? 22.

7. Strong disapprobation of their course=What shall I say to you? (A) shall I praise you in this? (B) I praise you not.

8. Justice of this censure evinced from the source and object of this supper=(A) For I received of the Lord that which also I delivered unto you, (a) how that the Lord Jesus in the night in which he was betrayed took bread; and when he had given thanks, he brake it, (b) and said, This is my body, which is for you : (c) this do in remembrance of me. (B) In like manner also (a) [he took] the cup, after supper, (b) saying, This cup is the new covenant in my blood : (c) this do, as oft as ye drink it, in remembrance of me. 23-25.

9. Explanatory comment=For as often as ye eat this bread, and drink the cup, ye proclaim the Lord's death till he come. 26.

10. Consequent inviolable sacrednes of the supper=Wherefore whosoever (A) shall eat the bread or drink the cup of the Lord unworthily, (B) shall be guilty of the body and the blood of the Lord. 27.

11. Resulting need of self-examination=(A) But let a man prove himself, (B) and so (a) let him eat of the bread, (b) and drink of the cup. 28.

12. Ground of this need=For he that eats and drinks (A) eats and drinks judgment unto himself, (B) if he discern not the body. 29.

13. Indication of this judgment=For this cause (A) many among you are weak and sickly, (B) and not a few sleep. 30.

14. The practical lesson hereby enforced=(A) But if we discerned ourselves, (B) we should not be judged. 31.

15. Object of this judgment=But when we are judged, (A) we are chastened of the Lord, (B) that we may not be condemned with the world. 32.

16. Consequent exhortation=Wherefore, my brethren, (A) when you come together to eat, wait one for another. (B) If any

man is hungry, let him eat at home; (A B) that your coming together be not unto judgment. 33, 34.

17.   General reference to other wrongs=And the rest, will I set in order whensoever I come. 34.

Queries.

(1).   How *must* there be heresies among them *that* the approved may be made manifest? 19.

Neither from the context nor from the force of the language employed is the supposition of any reference to a divine decree in the case justified, as Meyer and others suppose.   The impersonal verb translated *must* ranges in meaning all the way from rigid necessity to simple propriety.   As expressing the latter, notice its use in Luke xv. 32.   In the passage before us it denotes the practical consequence of an existing state of things as in Acts xiv. 22.   The conjunction translated *that* denotes here, as in many cases, simply the result as the legitimate outcome of the state of things at Corinth.   To suppose, as many exegetes do, that this conjunction always has the *telic* force denoting purpose, and never the *ecbatic* sense, signifying result, is in direct conflict with a multitude of passages.   And besides these passages which read as does Matt. i. 22, it would be absolutely absurd to represent this conjunction as denoting purpose or design in John ix. 2, and Rom. xi. 11.   The simple meaning of the passage before us is presented in the thought that Paul, considering the operation of influences and tendencies at work in the Corinthian church, reaches the conviction that they must, by this time, have produced heresies or factious divisions, so that those who are divinely approved become manifest as standing aloof from such evils.

(2).   What the discerning of the Lord's body? ver. 29.   *Cf.* 24.

(3).   What the judgment that the unworthy would drink unto themselves? ver. 29.   *Cf.* ver. 30–32.

(4).   What the important distinction, as seen in ver. 32, between corrective judgment and final condemnation?

SECTION SEVENTH.
The Nature and Utility of Spiritual Gifts.
xii. 1–xiv. 40.

¶ I. *Test of the Spirit's Presence as the Source of Its Various Gifts. xii. 1–3.*

1. Intimation of their need of enlightenment=Now concerning spiritual gifts, brethren, I would not have you ignorant. 1.

2. Ground of this need=Ye know that when ye were Gentiles (A) ye were led away unto those dumb idols, (B) as you happened to be led.* 2.

3. Consequent negative description of the Spirit's work in illumination=Wherefore I give you to understand, that no man speaking in the Spirit of God says, Jesus is anathema; 3.

4. The positive criterion in the case=and no man can say, Jesus is Lord, but in the Holy Spirit.

¶ II. *Manifold Operations of the Spirit with Oneness of Purpose and Aim. xii. 4–11.*

1. Mode of divine manifestation=(A) Now there are diversities of gifts, but the same Spirit. (B) And there are diversities of ministrations, and the same Lord. (C) And there are diversities of workings, but the same God, (C²) who works all things in all. 4–6.

2. Object of these operations=But to each one is given the manifestation of the Spirit to profit withal. 7.

3. Specification of these in their variety of form=(A) For to one is given through the Spirit the word of wisdom; (B) and to another the word of knowledge, according to the same Spirit: (C) to another faith, in the same Spirit; (D) and to another gifts of healings, in the one Spirit; (E) and to another workings of miracles; (F) and to another prophecy; (G) and to another discernings of spirits: (H) to another divers kinds of tongues; (I) and to another the interpretation of tongues: 8–10.

4. Re-affirmance of the relation of all these to the one Spirit as their source=(A) but all these works the one and the same Spirit, (B) dividing to each one severally even as he will. 11.

---

* Green's rendering of the last clause.

Queries.

(1). Distinguish between "the word of wisdom" and "the word of knowledge." ver. 8.

(2). Distinguish between the faith here said to be bestowed upon some, and Christian faith as possessed by all. ver. 9. *Cf.* xiii. 2; Matt. xvii. 20.

(3). Why the bestowment of these supernatural gifts upon the primitive churches?

The first form of the truth as it "is in Jesus," which we now have in the New Testament, was the oral form, and the churches stood in need of unerring guidance by the inspired apostles and prophets of the new kingdom. *They* were the New Testament to all believers till by them the books were written that now compose that infallible directory. Indeed, it was by the power of this divine truth upon the tongues of living men supernaturally illuminated that believers were made and churches were established. See Acts xxvi. 16–18. Thus it was first the truth, and then the church, and not as Rome would teach us, first the church and then the truth of the New Testament. Nor did the divine authority of the Gospels, the Book of Acts, the great Epistles of Paul and of other apostles depend on the collection of these Inspired Writings into one volume. The formation of the Canon did not *create* the New Testament, as another Romish deception represents. It existed before in its separately circulating infallible documents.

¶ III. *Correspondence between the Unity of the Spirit in the Variety of Its Gifts and the Unity of the Church in the Variety of Its Members. xii. 12–30.*

1. Analogy as to organic unity between the body and the church═(A) For as the body is one, (a) and has many members, (b) and all the members of the body, being many, are one body; (B) so also is Christ. 12.

2. This in keeping with the one divine source of this organic unity═(A) For in one Spirit were we all baptized into one body, (a) whether Jews or Greeks, (b) whether bond or free; (B) and were all made to drink of one Spirit. 13.

3. Justification of this variety in unity by analogy═For the [human] body (A) is not one member, (B) but many. 14.

4. Consequent lesson of contentment=(A) If the foot shall say, Because I am not the hand, I am not of the body; it is not therefore not of the body. (B) And if the ear shall say, Because I am not the eye, I am not of the body; it is not therefore not of the body. 15, 16.

5. Argument evincing the necessity of variety=(A) If the whole body were an eye, where were the hearing? (B) If the whole were hearing, where were the smelling? 17.

6. Consequent manifestation of divine wisdom in the case =But now has God set the members each one of them in the body, even as it pleased him? 18.

7. Necessity for this variety in organic unity re-asserted= (A) And if they were all one member, where were the body? (B) But now (a) they are many members, (b) but one body. 19, 20.

8. Consequent reciprocal need and dependence=(A) And the eye cannot say to the hand, I have no need of thee : (B) or again the head to the feet, I have no need of you. 21.

9. Further justification of this reciprocal relation=Nay, much rather, (A) those members of the body which seem to be more feeble are necessary : (B) and those members of the body which we think to be less honourable, upon these we bestow more abundant honour; (C) and our uncomely members have more abundant comeliness ; 22, 23.

10. Ground of this distinction in the distribution of regard =(A) whereas our comely members have no need : (B) but God tempered the body together, giving more abundant honour to that member which lacked ; 24.

11. The end in view=(A) that there should be no schism in the body; (B) but that the members should have the same care one for another. 25.

12. Consequent reciprocal sympathy established=(A) And whether one member suffers, all the members suffer with it ; (B) or one member is honoured, all the members rejoice with it. 26.

13. Spiritual application=(A) Now ye are the body of Christ, (B) and severally members thereof. 27.

14. The essential organic provisions of the spiritual body= And God has set some in the church, (A) first apostles, (B) secondly prophets, (C) thirdly teachers, (D) then miracles, (E) then gifts of healings, (F) helps, (G) governments, (H) divers kinds of tongues. 28.

15. Interrogative assertion of the necessity of this spiritual diversity=(A) Are all apostles? (B) are all prophets? (C) are all teachers? (D) are all workers of miracles? (E) have all gifts of healings? (F) do all speak with tongues? (G) do all interpret? 29, 30.

Queries.

(1). How in one Spirit were we all baptized into one body? 13.

(a). There can be no reference whatever to the baptism of the Holy Spirit which, as the record shows, subserved special ends and never *introduced any one into the body of Christ.* See Acts ii. 1–47, where the baptism of the Spirit was to qualify the apostles for their work, and Acts x. 1–48, where its object was to overcome Jewish opposition to the admission of Gentiles to the kingdom, in the demonstration of God's purpose to accept all upon the same conditions. In the latter case, so special was it and unexpected by Peter, that he says : "And I remembered the word of the Lord" concerning this baptism. (b). But the reference is to Christian baptism, through which, as led by the Spirit, believers are "baptized into Christ." Rom. vi. 3; Gal. iii. 27. The thought of Paul is that as the one Spirit was the source of all the gifts enumerated in the context, so he was the one source of the organic unity with the variety of functions established in the formation of the one body of Christ. See in the original the identity of construction in ver. 9 and ver. 13.

(2). How the uncomely members have more abundant comeliness? 23. *Cf.* ver. 24.

(3). How classify helps and "governments" with apostles, prophets, and teachers? 29.

Abstract for concrete as shown in ver. 28 as compared with 30.

¶ IV. *Contrast of a More Excellent Way with the Use of Spiritual Gifts. xii. 31–xiii. 13.*

1. Indication of a better way as superior to all gifts=(A) But desire earnestly the greater gifts. (B) And a still more excellent way shew I unto you. 31.

2. Its value negatively shown by its absence from the exercise of these gifts= (A) I am become sounding brass, or a clanging cymbal, (a) if I speak with the tongues of men and of angels

(b) but have not love : (b) and I am nothing, (a) if I have the gift of prophecy, and know all mysteries and all knowledge, and if I have all faith, so as to remove mountains ; (b) but have not love. 1, 2.

3. Its value negatively evinced still further by its absence from self-sacrifice=And it profits me nothing, (a) if I bestow all my goods to feed the poor, and if I give my body to be burned, (b) but have not love. 3.

4. Its value positively indicated by enumeration of its attributes=(a) Love suffers long, (a²) and is kind ; (b) love envies not ; (c) love vaunts not itself, (c²) is not puffed up, (d) does not behave itself unseemly, (e) seeks not its own, (f) is not provoked, (f²) takes not account of evil; (g) rejoices not in unrighteousness, (g²) but rejoices with the truth ; (h) bears all things, (i) believes all things, (j) hopes all things, (k) endures all things. 4–7.

5. Its superiority to spiritual gifts evinced by contrast of its perpetuity with their evanescence=(a) Love never fails ; (b) but (a) whether there be prophecies, they shall be done away ; (b) whether there be tongues, they shall cease ; (c) whether there be knowledge, it shall be done away. 8.

6. The wider underlying ground of this distinction=(a) For we know in part, (a²) and we prophesy in part : (b) but (a) when that which is perfect is come, (b) that which is in part shall be done away. 9, 10.

7. Illustration by analogy=(a) When I was a child, (a) I spake as a child, (b) I felt as a child, (c) I thought as a child : (b) now that I am become a man, (b²) I have put away childish things. 11.

8. Second figurative illustration=(a) For now we see in a mirror, darkly ; (b) but then face to face : 12.

9. Literal representation of the matter=(a) now I know in part ; (b) but then shall I know even as also I have been known.

10. Relative superiority of love as chief of the abiding principles=(a) But now abides faith, hope, love, (a²) these three ; (b) and the greatest of these is love. 13.

Queries.

(1). To what end is love "a still more excellent way" than spiritual gifts? 31. *Cf.* xiv. 12, 26.

(2). What the perfection to which reference is made in ver. 10?

The difference as seen in ver. 12 between Paul's own perfection hereafter and his partial realizations in the "now" of which he writes shows that the reference is to the eternal consummation in Christ.

(3) Why love represented as the greatest of the three abiding principles? *Cf.* description in ver. 4–7.

¶ V. *Superiority of Prophecy to the Gift of Tongues as Evinced from Their Comparative Utility.* xiv. 1–19.

1. Injunction as to the more important source of edification =Follow after love; 1.

2. Injunction as to the less=(A) yet desire earnestly spiritual gifts, (B) but rather that you may prophesy.

3. Ground of this preference of prophecy=(A) For he that speaks in a tongue (a) speaks not unto men, (b) but unto God; (a²) for no man understands; (b²) but in the spirit he speaks mysteries. (B) But he that prophesies (a) speaks unto men edification, (b) and comfort, (c) and consolation. 2, 3.

4. Consequent difference in effect=(A) He that speaks in a tongue edifies himself; (B) but he that prophesies edifies the church. 4.

5. His comparative estimate of the two gifts repeated=(A) Now I would have you all speak with tongues, (B) but rather that you should prophesy : (B²) and greater is he that prophesies than he that speaks with tongues, 5.

6. The only consideration that would remove the latter's inferiority=except he interpret, that the church may receive edifying.

7. Justification of this instruction=But now, brethren, if I come unto you speaking with tongues, (A) what shall I profit you, (B) unless I speak to you (a) either by way of revelation, (b) or of knowledge, (a²) or of prophesying, (b²) or of teaching? 6.

8. Illustration═Even things without life, giving a voice, whether pipe or harp, (A) if they give not a distinction in the sounds, how shall it be known what is piped or harped? 7.

9. Second illustrative example═(A) For if the trumpet give an uncertain voice, (B) who shall prepare himself for war? 8.

10. Application═So also you, (A) unless you utter by the tongue speech easy to be understood, (B) how shall it be known what is spoken? (B²) for you will be speaking into the air. 9.

11. Illustration continued═There are, it may be, so many kinds of voices in the world, and no kind is without signification. (A) If then I know not the meaning of the voice, (B) I shall be to him that speaks a barbarian, * and he that speaks will be a barbarian unto me. 10, 11.

12. Hortatory application═So also you, since you are zealous of spiritual gifts, seek that you may abound unto the edifying of the church. 12.

13. Consequent advice═Wherefore let him that speaks in a tongue pray that he may interpret. 13.

14. Ground of this advice═For if I pray in a tongue, (A) my spirit prays, (B) but my understanding is unfruitful. 14.

15. Practical conclusion═What is it then? (A) I will pray with the spirit, (B) and I will pray with the understanding also: (A²) I will sing with the spirit, (B²) and I will sing with the understanding also. 15.

16. Argument justifying this═Else if thou bless with the spirit, (A) how shall he that fills the place of the unlearned say the Amen at thy giving of thanks, (B) seeing he knows not what thou sayest? 16.

17. The argument continued═(A) For thou verily givest thanks well, (B) but the other is not edified. 17.

18. Final emphasis of the preference for prophecy without depreciating the gift of tongues═(A) I thank God, I speak with tongues more than you all: (B) howbeit in the church I would rather speak five words with my understanding, that I might instruct others also, than ten thousand words in a tongue. 18, 19.

Queries.

(1). What common weakness is illustrated by the Corinthian preference of tongues to prophecy?

---
* Foreigner.

The disposition to choose what is striking and showy rather than that which may further the spiritual interests of men. It was in keeping with the Grecian fondness for "excellency of speech" and of human "wisdom" which were ignored by Paul in his preaching. ii. 1-5.

(2). What the distinction between revelation and knowledge, prophesying and teaching? ver. 6.

Revelation is the matter supernaturally communicated by prophesying, and knowledge, as here conceived, is the matter ordinarily communicated by teaching. Edification results from both and they stand thus in contrast with speech unintelligible and unprofitable.

(3). How sing and pray "with the understanding" as well as "with the spirit"? ver. 15.

Correct here a prevalent error by comparing ver. 16-19.

(4). What practice in Romish worship is condemned by the teaching of this paragraph?

¶ VI. *Comparison of Prophecy and the Gift of Tongues in the Light of the Specific Object of Each. xiv. 20-25.*

1. The apostle solicits enlightened consideration of the subject=Brethren, (a) be not children in mind : (b) howbeit in malice be you babes, (a²) but in mind be men. 20.

2. Scriptural citation presenting the ground of his argument=In the law it is written, (a) By men of strange tongues and by the lips of strangers will I speak unto this people; (b) and not even thus will they hear me, says the Lord. 21.

3. A distinction thus suggested=(a) Wherefore tongues are for a sign, (a) not to those who believe, (b) but to the unbelieving : (b) but prophesying is for a sign, (a) not to the unbelieving, (b) but to those who believe. 22.

4. Consequent difference of result from a practical test of each=If therefore the whole church be assembled together, (a) and all speak with tongues, (a) and there come in men unlearned * or unbelieving, (b) will they not say that you are mad? (b) But if all prophesy, (a) and there come in one unbelieving or unlearned, (b) he is convicted by all, (b²) he is judged by all; 24.

---

* That is, "unlearned," in the language employed.

5. Ulterior results of this effect of prophesying=the secrets of his heart are made manifest; (A) and so he will fall down on his face, (A²) and worship God, (B) declaring that God is among you indeed. 25.

Queries.

(1). How unbelievers convicted and judged through prophesying so as to make manifest the secrets of the heart? 24, 25. See Heb. iv. 12 and compare Acts ii. 37 with Acts ii. 12, 13, to see the difference between this effect and that of the mere use of tongues.

(2). What lesson to be deduced from the ground of Paul's preference of prophesying to speaking in tongues?

¶ VII. *Regulations Respecting the Use of Spiritual Gifts and the Conduct of Public Worship. xiv. 26–40.*

1. Summary of gifts bestowed on the Corinthians=What is it then, 'brethren? When you come together, (A) each' one has a psalm, (B) has a teaching, (C) has a revelation, (D) has a tongue, (E) has an interpretation. 26.

2. General direction as to the use of these=Let all things be done unto edifying.

3. Special direction as to speaking in a tongue=If any man speaks in a tongue, (A) let it be (a) by two, (b) or at the most by three, (a b) and that in turn; (B) and let one interpret: 27.

4. The instruction modified in view of a change of circumstances=but if there be no interpreter, (A) let him keep silence in the church; (B) and let him speak (a) to himself, (b) and to God. 28.

5. Special direction as to prophesying=(A) And let the prophets speak (a) by two (b) or three, (B) and let the others discern. 29.

6. Modification of this to suit emergency=(A) But if a revelation be made to another sitting by, (B) let the first keep silence. 30.

7. The observance of these instructions set forth as practicable=(A) For you all can prophesy one by one, (a) that all may learn, (b) and all may be comforted; (B) and the spirits of the prophets are subject to the prophets; 31, 32.

8. Explanatory reason=(A) for God (a) is not a God of confusion, (b) but of peace; (B) as in all the churches of the saints. 33.

9. Prophesying or teaching in the assembly disallowed to women=(A) Let the women keep silence in the churches : (A²) for it is not permitted unto them to speak; (B) but let them be in subjection, (B²) as also says the law. 34.

10. Extension of the prohibition to the public asking of questions for instruction=And if they would learn anything, let them ask their own husbands at home : 35.

11. Reason=for it is shameful for a woman to speak in the church.

12. Argument against this Corinthian innovation=What? (A) was it from you that the word of God went forth? (B) or came it unto you alone? 36.

13. The challenge of a true test for determining the authority of his instructions=(A) If any man thinks himself to be a prophet, or spiritual, (a) let him take knowledge of the things which I write unto you, (b) that they are the commandment of the Lord. (B) But if any man is ignorant, let him be ignorant. 37, 38.

14. Final hortatory conclusion from the whole argument as to prophecy and the use of tongues=Wherefore, my brethren, (A) desire earnestly to prophesy, (B) and forbid not to speak with tongues. 39.

15. General concluding direction=But let all things be done decently and in order. 40.

Queries.

(1). Show how ver. 34 and xi. 5 can stand together under the "Law of Harmony."

(a). If by implication the apostle grants to the Corinthian women the privilege of prophesying in the public assembly in xi. 5, a practice which in xiv. 34, he clearly forbids in their case, at least, if not as to other Christian women, there is no harmony but conflict between the two passages. The Law of Harmony which enforces the recognition of the unity of divine truth thus precludes such interpretation of xi. 5. (b). On examination it is clear that a different question is under consideration in each passage from that which is handled in the other. The *manner of procedure* in the public prophesying of women is considered in one case and the *merits of the practice itself* come up for decision in the other.

Thus Paul by not raising the question in xi. 5 which he decides in xiv. 34 only *apparently* allows in the one passage what he emphatically prohibits in the other, precisely as he had dealt with the question of eating sacrificial meat at an idol's table in viii. 9, 10 as compared with x. 19–21.

(2). What evidence that Paul did not limit the prohibition of ver. 34 to any people or any age? 34.

(a). He gives similar instruction to Timothy as an evangelist to regulate his course in the matter wherever he might go. *Cf.* I. Tim. ii. 11, 12. (b). In the passage in hand he justifies the prohibition by saying "as also says the law" which all exegetes, we believe, regard, and very justly, as a reference to Gen. iii. 16 where the Creator is adjusting the relation of the sexes for all time in organizing the human family as represented by the first pair. Woman was to stand by man's side on the same social and spiritual plane while headship was assigned to him and a subordinate sphere allotted to her. This is the "ruling" to which reference is made and experience attests the divine wisdom of the arrangement. (c). His argumentative protest against this Corinthian innovation in ver. 36 implies the universally recognized propriety of his teaching in the case. "What? was it from you that the word of God went forth? or came it unto you alone"? This is finely paraphrased by Kling as follows : "Are you the original church, so that your wisdom is to set the standard of propriety ; or are you the only church, so that you are at liberty to stand alone by yourselves and your own conceits"? (d). If as the majority of the finest modern critics decide that according to the sense the last clause of ver. 33 should stand connected with ver. 34, the universal Christian recognition of the propriety of the prohibition, in that age, at least, is clearly attested. It would then read : "*As in all the churches of the saints*, let *your* women," etc. Let me say, that so perfectly manifest is the meaning of Paul that only those who take offense at his teaching on this subject will, on the one hand, resort to unhermeneutical methods and sophistical arts to evade the force of his language ; or, on the other hand, indulge in unworthy flings at the apostle himself. And now shall we apologize for this teaching of an inspired apostle of the infallible Christ who in the exercise of divine wisdom called and qualified this grandest of human teachers to illumine the world by turning

men "from darkness to light, and from the power of Satan unto
God"?   We may do so whenever it can be shown that the spirit
of any age is superior to the Spirit of God.

(3).   What the implied contrast in ver. 37, 38 between
apostolic authority and rationalistic arrogance?

As heretofore seen, there were those at Corinth who, "puffed
up" with the conceit of their own wisdom, presumed, like many
in our day, to sit in judgment upon Paul's religious instructions.
The capacity to thus judge, we are assured in these verses, implies
the possession of the prophetic Spirit as of one who is "spiritual,"
or inspired.   In that case, says the apostle, they will "take
knowledge of the things which I write unto you, *that they are
the commandment of the Lord.*"   "But if any man is ignorant,"
of this fact, not discerning the true source of this divine teaching,
let him be content with this ignorance and pretend not to be a
competent judge in the case.

SECTION EIGHTH.
The Resurrection of the Dead.
xv. 1–58.
¶ I. *Ground of the Argument. xv. 1–11.*

1.   Attention directed to the gospel as the source of all spiritual character and life=Now I make known unto you, brethren,
the gospel which I preached unto you, (A) which also you
received, (B) wherein also you stand, (C) by which also you are
saved; 1, 2.

2.   Conditions of this spiritual result=(A) if you hold fast
what I preached unto you, * (B) except you believed in vain. 2.

3.   The elementary gospel facts on which this saving power
depends=For I delivered unto you first of all that which also I
received, (A) how that Christ died for our sins according to the
Scriptures; (B) and that he was buried; (C) and that he has been
raised on the third day according to the Scriptures; 3, 4.

4.   Proof of the crowning fact of this gospel of Christ=(A)
and that he appeared to Cephas; (B) then to the twelve; (C)
then he appeared to above five hundred brethren at once, (a) of
whom the greater part remain until now, (b) but some are fallen
asleep; (D) then he appeared to James : (E) then to all the apostles ;

---

* Marginal reading preferred.

(F) and last of all, as unto one born out of due time, he
appeared to me also. 5–8.

    5. Parenthetical explanation of this description of himself
=(A) For I am the least of the apostles, (B) that am not meet
to be called an apostle, (B²) because I persecuted the church of
God. 9.

    6. Consequent indication of the gracious source of his
efficiency=But by the grace of God I am what I am : 10.

    7. Result of this gracious visitation=(A) and his grace
which was bestowed upon me was not found vain; (B) but I
laboured more abundantly than they all :

    8. Explanation=(A) yet not I, (B) but the grace of God
which was with me.

    9. The gracious result=Whether then it be I or they, (A)
so we preach, (B) and so you believed. 11.

Queries.

    (1). Why say that the Corinthians were saved by the gos-
pel "except" they had *"believed in vain"*? 2. *Cf.* ver. 14.

    (2). Is Christ's death an element of the *gospel*, or *good news
to mankind*, in that he simply died, or in that *he died for our
sins*? 3. *Cf.* I. Pet. ii. 24 and Is. liii. 4–8.

    (3). Why speak of this as *"according to the Scriptures"*?
3, 4. Compare Acts ii. 23 and see that the death of Jesus was no
needless accident.

    (4). Show that the character of the testimony concerning
the risen Christ was such as to utterly preclude self-deception in
the witnesses.

    As seen in ver. 5–8; I. Jno. i. 1–3; Jno. xx. 24–29, the res
urrection of Christ was attested by a plurality of the senses of a
plurality of witnesses on a plurality of occasions. Hence, the
apostles gave their testimony to the world without the shadow of
a doubt upon their souls as to its truthfulness and encountered
every form of persecution in its behalf with unfaltering confidence and the utmost composure. They were not credulous
dupes to be blindly led by "cunningly devised fables" and accordingly in the first place demanded the kind of evidence above
described. "Except I shall see *in his hands the print of the*

nails," says Thomas, "and *put my finger* into the *print* of *the nails*, and *put* my *hand* into *his side, I will not believe*,"—*and he was right*. "That which we have heard, that which we have seen with our eyes, that which we beheld, and our hands handled, * * declare we unto you," says the apostle John. Jesus wanted just such witnesses so that when they stood up before men in his name they might know whereof they spoke and bear their testimony concerning him with the absolute certainty of its truth.

(5). What does Paul mean by saying that he among the apostolic witnesses was "as one born out of due time"? 8.

Interpret in the light of the explanatory reason given in ver 9 and correct a common mistake.

(6). What the "grace" to which he here refers as bestowed upon him? ver. 10. Notice the context and compare as parallel Eph. iii. 2, 7, 8.

¶ II. *The Essential Connection between Christ's Resurrection and the Resurrection of the Dead in General. xv. 12-19.*

1. Inconsistency of some of the Corinthian believers=Now if Christ is preached that he has been raised from the dead, how say some among you that there is no resurrection of the dead? 12.

2. Folly of this denial evinced by a conditional "sorites"= (A) But if there is no resurrection of the dead, (B) neither has Christ been raised: (B²) and if Christ has not been raised, (C) then (a) is our preaching vain, (b) your faith also is vain. 13, 14.

3. Additional absurdity involved in this denial=Yea, and we are found false witnesses of God; 15.

4. Proof that such would be the consequence=(A) because we witnessed of God that he raised up Christ: (B) whom (a) he raised not up, (b) if so be that the dead are not raised.

5. Substantial repetition of the conditional argument=(A) For if the dead are not raised, (B) neither has Christ been raised: (B²) and if Christ has not been raised, (a) your faith is vain; (b) you are yet in your sins. 16, 17.

6. Additional absurdity involved=Then they also who are fallen asleep in Christ have perished. 18.

7. General unhappy result that would follow=If in this life only we have hoped in Christ, we are of all men most pitiable. 19.

Queries.

(1). How does the denial of the general resurrection imply the denial of Christ's resurrection, and, *per contra*, how does the proof of his resurrection imply the certainty of the general resurrection?

Not only is the power that raised him from the dead *adequate* to the resurrection of all, but its actual exertion in his case is a *guarantee*, according to ver. 20–22, that it will be exerted in the resurrection of all; since the whole significance and design of his resurrection was the overthrow of the dominion of death in the interests of humanity. This most stupendous of all events, this overwhelming and imperishable fact, is the blazing sun of human history before the consuming glance of which the mists and fogs of all unbelief are destined to vanish away.

(2). How would believers be yet in their sins, if Christ was not raised from the dead? 17.

(3). How be "of all men most pitiable"? 19. *Cf.* ver. 31, 32.

¶ III. *Blissful Results of Christ's Resurrection as an Established Fact in Contrast with the Consequences of Unbelief above Specified. xv. 20–28.*

1. Positive affirmation based on the testimony submitted in ver. 5–8=(A) But now has Christ been raised from the dead, (B) the firstfruits of those who are asleep. 20.

2. Ground of this relation of Christ's resurrection to the general resurrection=(A) For since by man came death, (B) by man came also the resurrection of the dead. (A²) For as in Adam all die, (B²) so also in Christ shall all be made alive. 21, 22.

3. The chronological order explained=But each in his own order: (A) Christ the firstfruits; (B) then they that are Christ's, at his coming. 23.

4. The ultimate result=Then comes the end, (A) when he shall deliver up the kingdom to God, even the Father; (B) when he shall have abolished (a) all rule (b) and all authority (c) and power. (B²). For he must reign, till he has put all his enemies under his feet. 24, 25.

5. The final conquest of death thus implied=(A) The last enemy that shall be abolished is death. (B) For, He put all things in subjection under his feet. 26, 27.

6. The only limit to this subjugation=(A) But when he says, All things are put in subjection, (B) it is evident that he is excepted who did subject all things unto him. 27.

7. Final position of the Son himself=(A) And when all things have been subjected unto him, (B) then shall the Son also himself be subjected to him that did subject all things unto him, 28.

8. Resulting consummation in the universal recognition of divine sovereignty=that God may be all in all.

Queries.

(1). What figure used and what its full force in the representation of Christ risen as "the firstfruits of those who are asleep"? 20.

(2). How "in Christ shall all be made alive"? 22.

Note the connection between this and the verse preceding and compare Jno. v. 28, 29.

(3). How the Son to be in the end made subject unto the Father? 28.

This is a theme too lofty for us to handle except to the extent that we are guided and enlightened by the word of God. That Paul could deal with the subject in the positive terms and confident manner here indicated is evidence of his inspiration. *We* must thankfully accept what knowledge we may gather from the infallible teaching of those who are thus supernaturally illumined. And in relation to the matter before us let us not forget that the human in Jesus remains, though glorified in his exaltation to the very throne of the Father. This would of itself suggest the Son's subordination in some way to the God and Father of all. And what we may learn from the divine word is that such a subordinate position of the Son is compatible with the divine *oneness* and *equality* of the Father and the Son, so clearly taught in such passages as Jno. x. 30-33; xiv. 9-11 ; Philippians ii. 5-8.

¶ IV. *Completion of This Grand Argument by Showing the
Conduct of Christ's Witnesses to be Inexplicable, if
There be No Resurrection. xv. 29–34.*
   1. Argument from their sufferings and martyrdom=Else
(A) what shall they do who are baptized for the dead? * (A²) If
the dead are not raised at all, why then are they baptized for
them? (B) why do we also stand in jeopardy every hour? 29, 30.
   2. Evidence of this jeopardy=I protest by that glorying in
you, brethren, which I have in Christ Jesus our Lord, I die daily.
31.
   3. This exemplified and expanded into an argument=(A)
If after the manner of men I fought with beasts at Ephesus, what
does it profit me? (B) If the dead are not raised, (a) let us eat
and drink, (b) for to-morrow we die. 32.
   4. Warning against the corrupting influence of rationalistic
deniers of the resurrection=Be not deceived : Evil company does
corrupt good manners. 33.
   5. Exhortation to free themselves from the practical effect
of this influence=(A) Awake up righteously, (B) and sin not;
34.
   6. Ground of the exhortation=for some have no knowledge
of God :
   7. Motive in giving it=I speak this to move you to shame.
                        Queries.
   (1). What insuperable objections to the view, generally
adopted by exegetes, that the baptism to which reference is made
in ver. 29 was a custom according to which living persons were
baptized for persons who had died? 29.
   (a). Not a trace of such a practice can be found in Church
History till the fifth century and then only in an obscure subdi-
vision of the sect of the Marcionites who evidently based their
superstitious custom upon a misunderstanding of the passage before
us. Consult Neander's Church History vol. I. p. 478. (b). Had
such a miserable perversion of baptism existed at Corinth or elsewhere in Paul's day it is inconceivable that while giving needed
instructions and exposing errors in doctrine and practice he would
have failed to denounce this one as vigorously as he opposed the
perversion of the Lord's supper and other abuses, and certainly

---

* Better rendered "baptized in reference to the dead." Well rendered by Green; "baptized concerning the dead."

would not have appeared to sanction it by using it in his argument. (c). And it is equally inconceivable that this great master of logic could have supposed for one moment that this silly practice could aid him in overwhelmingly demonstrating the all-important spiritual truth in which the whole human race is vitally interested. Not even as a supposed *argumentum ad hominem*, would such reference be of any conceivable value or rise to the dignity of the subject and the occasion.

(2). What grounds for regarding it as a reference to the baptism of martyrdom, so named and predicted by Jesus in Mark к. 39?

(a). First of all the distinction between the "they" who were undergoing this baptism and the "we" who were not as yet but were in "jeopardy" of it "every hour." And it is especially worthy of note that in the original the pronoun itself, for "we" is used emphasizing the distinction and clearly showing that the "we" had not as yet participated in the baptism to which reference is made but were hourly exposed to it. (b). The use of the term "jeopardy" clearly points to something calamitous connected with this baptism and this idea is developed in ver. 30–32 in which Paul speaks of virtually dying daily through his exposure to persecution so that the drift of thought in the context justifies our exposition. (c). Not only would such a reference to the baptism of martyrdom with the connected sufferings on the part of Christ's witnesses have logical force as an element of Paul's great argument on the grand theme under consideration, but, as we shall see, this link of the logical chain here presented is indispensable to a complete demonstration for all ages.

(3). What bearing on the exegesis of the passage has the adjunct here translated, "for the dead"?

Whether the phrase in the original should be represented by this expression or be rendered otherwise depends altogether on the subject-matter and the general sequence of thought. The preposition in the case when used with the genitive, as it is here, often "signifies, in general, *in reference to, as to,* a matter." (Winer.) Whether or not it has this meaning in any given instance depends, of course, on the demands of the context and circumstances bearing on the case. Now we have already seen that according to these, the phrase "baptized for the dead" is meaningless in the passage before us. How will the rendering, "baptized in reference to the dead" meet the requirements to which reference is made? Let us keep in mind that if there is any benefit whatever arising from the baptism of martyrdom and hence any sense in undergoing such baptism or subjecting one's self to the "jeopardy" of it, this benefit appertains to those who are in the realm of death and stands not among the advantages of this life, since these are all surrendered in this act. It is therefore a baptism "in reference to the dead" touching the question of advantage or benefit in the case and Paul says very truly, that it is a senseless sacrifice of life, if there is no resurrection. If "I fought with beasts at Ephesus, what does it profit me? If the dead are not raised, let us eat and drink, for to-morrow we die." 32.

(4). In what sense did Paul fight with beasts (literally have a beast fight) at Ephesus? 32.

Consider this in view of the privileges connected with his Roman citizenship.

(5). What bearing has the reference to the sufferings of Christ's witnesses, in ver. 29-31, upon the Corinthian denial of the resurrection? 29-31. *Cf.* ver. 15.

If they were right in their denial, the apostles and others would be "found false witnesses." The proof therefore of their trustworthiness is a refutation of their skepticism.

(6). Give now in regular order the several links in this unanswerable chain of reasoning in proof of the resurrection.

(A). HYPOTHETICALLY STATED.

(a). If there is no resurrection of the dead, neither has Christ been raised. ver. 13. (b). If Christ has not been raised, the apostles and others were "false witnesses." ver. 15. (c). If they were false witnesses, why stood they "in jeopardy every hour"?* ver. 30.

---

* Note.—This question has never been answered by unbelievers, and never can be. Hence, the apostle's argument is of incalculable value to the Christian world in all ages.

(B). CATEGORICALLY STATED.

(a). The sufferings and martyrdom of Christ's witnesses fully established their trustworthiness. (b). Their testimony as trustworthy witnesses established the fact of Christ's resurrection. (c). The established fact of his resurrection involves the certainty of the general resurrection.

¶ V.   *Consideration of Objections Suggested by the Dissolution of the body.   xv. 35-49.*

1. Objections presented=But some one will say, (A) How are the dead raised? (B) and with what manner of body do they come? 35.

2. The objector's folly evinced by showing the relation of dissolution to revival=Thou foolish one, that which thou thyself sowest is not quickened, except it die: 36.

3. The body as raised shown under this analogy to be different from the body as sown=and that which thou sowest, (A) thou sowest not the body that shall be, (B) but a bare grain, (a) it may chance of wheat, (b) or of some other kind; 37.

4. Further explanation of the kind of body raised=(A) but God gives it a body even as it pleased him, (B) and to each seed a body of its own. 38.

5. Extension of the illustration as to the difference between the body as it is and as it shall be=All flesh is not the same flesh: (A) but there is one flesh of men, (B) and another flesh of beasts, (c) and another flesh of birds, (D) and another of fishes. 39.

6. Illustration by differences in the material universe=There are also celestial bodies, and bodies terrestrial: (A) but the glory of the celestial is one, (B) and the glory of the terrestrial is another. 40.

7. Narrowing the sphere of illustration to celestial bodies there are still differences of glory=(A) There is one glory of the sun, (B) and another glory of the moon, (c) and another glory of the stars; 41.

8. And differences even as to the stars=for one star differs from another star in glory.

9. Application connecting identity with diversity=So also is the resurrection of the dead. (A) (a) It is sown in corruption; (b) it is raised in incorruption: (B) (a) it is sown in dishonour;

(b) it is raised in glory : (c) (a) it is sown in weakness; (b) it is raised in power : (D) (a) it is sown a natural body; (b) it is raised a spiritual body. 42–44.

10.   Justification of this contrast=(A) If * there is a natural body, (B) there is also a spiritual body. 44.

11.   Further illustration and confirmation of the contrast= (A) So also it is written, The first man Adam became a living soul.   (B) The last Adam became a life-giving spirit. 45.

12.   The order of existence in the case=(A) Howbeit that is not first which is spiritual, (B) but that which is natural; (A²) then that which is spiritual. 46.

13.   Fundamental difference between the two Adamic heads of these two kinds of existence=(A) The first man is of the earth, earthy : (B) the second man is of heaven. 47.

14.   Conformity of each kind to its representative head= (A) As is the earthy, such are they also that are earthy : (B) and as is the heavenly, such are they also that are heavenly. 48.

15.   Consequent expectation of a spiritual and a glorified body in the resurrection=(A) And as we have borne the image of the earthy, (B) we shall also bear the image of the heavenly. 49.

Queries.

(1).   Show from ver. 42–44 that the resurrection concerns *the body* and not, as some have thought, the exit of the soul from the body at death. See also Philippians iii. 21.

(2).   Expose the false application often made of the statement respecting the difference of glory among the stars. 41.

Notice the question in ver. 35 that the whole paragraph is intended to answer and examine the whole drift of illustrative thought.

¶   VI. *Further Elucidation of Future Glorification by the Change to be Effected in the Bodies of Living Saints at the End of Time. xv. 50–58.*

1.   Necessity for a radical change asserted=Now this I say, brethren, (A) that flesh and blood cannot inherit the kingdom of God ; (B) neither does corruption inherit incorruption. 50.

2.   Consequent announcement of divine purpose in the case =Behold, I tell you a mystery : (A) We shall not all sleep, (B)

"If"=as certain as.

but we shall all be changed, (a) in a moment, (a²) in the twink-
ling of an eye, (b) at the last trumpet : 51, 52.

3. Confirmatory repetition=for the trumpet shall sound,
(A) and the dead shall be raised incorruptible, (B) and we shall
be changed. 52.

4. Retroversion to the necessity for this change=(A) For
this corruptible must put on incorruption, (B) and this mortal
must put on immortality. 53.

5. Resulting fulfilment of Scripture=(A) But when (a) this
corruptible shall have put on incorruption, (b) and this mortal shall
have put on immortality, (B) then shall come to pass the saying
that is written, (B²) Death is swallowed up in victory. 54.

6. Exulting outburst of Christian joy over this=(A) O death,
where is thy victory? (B) O death, where is thy sting? 55.

7. The original source of the dominion thus overthrown=
(A) The sting of death is sin ; (B) and the power of sin is the
law : 56.

8. The source of victory in the case pointed out with
thanksgiving=but thanks be to God who gives us the victory
through our Lord Jesus Christ. 57.

9. Consequent encouraging exhortation=Wherefore, my
beloved brethren, (A) be you stedfast, (A²) immoveable, (B)
always abounding in the work of the Lord, 58.

10. Sustaining reason for this course=forasmuch as you
know that your labour is not in vain in the Lord.

Queries.

(1). Show from ver. 53 that our bodies are not left to decay
and only the spirit survives. 53.

(2). How represent "the law" as "the power of sin"? ver.
56. *Cf.* Rom. vii. 7 ; Gal. iii. 10.

SECTION NINTH.

CONCLUSION OF THE EPISTLE WITH VARIOUS DIRECTIONS,
ADMONITIONS AND SALUTATIONS.
xvi. 1–24.

¶ I. *Instructions Concerning the Collection for the Poor Saints
in Judæa. xvi. 1–4.*

¶ II. *Reference to a Visit to the Corinthians Soon to be Made
by the Apostle. xvi. 5–9.*

¶ III. *Personal Allusion to Timothy and Apollos. xvi. 10–12.*

¶ IV. *General Exhortations. xvi. 13, 14.*

¶ V. *Special Intreaty Concerning Stephanas and Others.*

xvi. 15–18.

¶ VI. *Concluding Salutations. xvi. 19–24.*

ANALYSIS

OF

SECOND CORINTHIANS

SECTION FIRST.

PAUL'S VINDICATION OF HIS APOSTOLIC CHARACTER AND
COURSE OF LIFE ACCOMPANIED WITH EARNEST
APPEALS AND ADMONITIONS.

i. 1–vii. 16.

¶ I. *The Apostolic Greeting. i. 1, 2.*

1. Writer described=Paul, (A) an apostle of Jesus Christ
(B) through the will of God, 1.

2. His associate in the writing=and Timothy our brother,

3. The persons addressed=(A) unto the church of God which
is at Corinth, (B) with all the saints which are in the whole of
Achaia :

4. Benediction=Grace to you and peace (A) from God our
Father (B) and the Lord Jesus Christ. 2.

¶ II. *Introductory Reflections Touching the Twofold Fellowship of Christians in Suffering and in Comfort. i. 3–11*

1. Outburst of praise=Blessed be the God and Father of our
Lord Jesus Christ, 3.

2. Beneficent character of God which elicited this praise=
(A) the Father of mercies (B) and God of all comfort ;

3. The apostle's experience of this blessing=who comforts
us in all our affliction, 4.

4. End thereby subserved=(A) that we may be able to comfort those who are in any affliction, (B) through the comfort wherewith we ourselves are comforted of God.

5. Ground of this fellowship=(A) For as the sufferings of
Christ abound unto us, (B) even so our comfort also abounds through
Christ. 5.

6. Extension of the benefit in both ways to the Corinthians
=(A) But whether we be afflicted, it is for your comfort and salvation ; (B) or whether we be comforted, it is for your comfort,

7. Power of this blessing described=which works in the patient enduring of the same sufferings which we also suffer :

8. Consequent hope of the apostle with reference to the Corinthians=and our hope for you is stedfast ; 7.

9. Explicit statement of the ground of this hope=knowing that, (A) as you are partakers of the sufferings, (B) so also are you of the comfort.

10. Reference to the special occasion suggestive of these reflections=For we would not have you ignorant, brethren, concerning our affliction which befell us in Asia, 8.

11. Intensity of this affliction described=(A) that we were weighed down exceedingly, (A²) beyond our power, (B) insomuch that we despaired even of life :

12. The end thus gained=yea, we ourselves have had the answer of death within ourselves, (A) that we should not trust in ourselves, (B) but in God who raises the dead : 9.

13. This trust justified by the result=who (A) delivered us out of so great a death, (B) and will deliver : 10.

14. This a ground of hope for the future=on whom we have set our hope that he will also still deliver us ;

15. Intercessory help of the Corinthians asked for the realization of this hope=ye also helping together on our behalf by your supplication ; 11.

16. Important result to follow=that, (A) for the gift bestowed upon us by means of many; (B) thanks may be given by many persons on our behalf.

Queries.

(1). How speak of God as "Father of mercies"? 3.

It cannot be regarded as a Hebraistic form of expression for "merciful Father" or, as some exegetes suppose, a case of the genitive of quality or attribute as we have the word mercy in the plural. It is metaphorical and represents God as the author or source of all mercies, similar to the representation of him as "the Father of lights" in Jas. i. 17.

(2). What comfort in Paul's case to which reference is made? 4. Cf. vii. 4-7.

(3). How "sufferings of Christ abound unto us"? 5. Cf. Rom. viii. 17; Philippians iii. 10; I. Pet. iv. 1, 12, 13.

(4.).   What affliction of Paul the occasion of these reflections?
8.

No personal exposure in the tumult at Ephesus, as far as the
record goes, answers to the description of this affliction given in
ver. 8–10.   It must therefore be one of those numerous afflictions
of Paul, not recorded, to which reference is made further on in
this Epistle, reducing him to hopeless extremity as to this life.

¶ III. *Integrity of His Course and Consistency of His Purposes and Plans Respecting the Corinthians. i. 12–22.*

1.   Ground of his claim to their helpful regard=For our
glorying is this, the testimony of our conscience, 12.

2.   Purport of this testimony=that we behaved ourselves in
the world, and more abundantly to you-ward; (A) in holiness
and sincerity of God, (B) not in fleshly wisdom, (A²) but in the
grace of God.

3.   This sincerity ascribed to his writings=For we write none
other things unto you, (A) than what you read (B) or even
acknowledge, 13.

4.   His hope of the continuance of past acknowledgment=
(A) and I hope you will acknowledge unto the end: (B) as you
did acknowledge us in part, 13, 14.

5.   Purport of this acknowledgment=that, in the day of
our Lord Jesus, (A) we are your glorying, (B) even as you also
are ours.

6.   His plans sincere as determined by this confident view=
And in this confidence I was minded (A) to come before unto you,
(B) that you might have a second benefit; (A²) and by you to
pass into Macedonia, (B²) and again from Macedonia to come unto
you, (C) and of you to be set forward on my journey unto Judæa.
15, 16.

7.   Consequent denial of vacillation and inconsistency=
When I therefore was thus minded, (A) did I show fickleness?
(B) or the things that I purpose, do I purpose according to the
flesh, (B²) that with me (a) there should be the yea yea (b) and
the nay nay? 17.

8.   His sincere consistency in preaching an argument evincing the same in conduct=But as God is faithful, our word toward
you is not yea and nay. 18.

9.   The argument more fully developed=For the Son of God,
Jesus Christ, (A) who was preached among you by us, (A²) even

by me and Silvanus and Timothy, (b) was (a) not yea and nay, (b) but in him is yea. 19.

10. This verified in the fulfilment of the promises=For how many soever be the promises of God, in him is the yea : 20.

11. Consequent propriety of their acceptance of his preaching=wherefore also (a) through him is the Amen, (b) unto the glory of God through us.

12. Additional proof of his consistency=Now he is God, (a) who establishes us with you in Christ, (b) and anointed us ; 21.

13. The argument expanded=(a) who also sealed us, (b) and gave us the earnest of the Spirit in our hearts. 22.

Queries.

(1). How have "a second benefit"? 15. Cf. 16.

According to his first plan of visitation he expected to go by way of Corinth into Macedonia and return from Macedonia to Corinth. The Corinthians would thus have "a second benefit" from his ministrations in carrying out that plan.

(2). What "word" of the apostle "toward" the Corinthians was "not yea and nay"? 18. Cf. 19.

The connection between these two verses shows that reference is made to the word preached concerning Christ Jesus and he argues that as his preaching to them was in all sincerity, so might naturally be regarded all of his expressed purposes concerning them.

(3). How in Christ is "the yea" of all the promises of God? 20.

The judaizers, against whom Paul's reasoning in this Epistle is chiefly directed, might see "the yea" of fulfilment of all the promises concerning Israel, but they virtually regarded divine promises as "nay" for all of the uncircumcised. With Paul the promises of God were all "yea" where Gentiles as well as Jews were embraced. In Christ is full salvation for all who accept him.

(4). What the consequent "Amen" which is "through him"?

"Amen" is approval or acknowledgment. The "yea" of the gospel preached by Paul was its absolute certainty, but its blessing is assured only to those who give to it the "Amen" of a practical acknowledgment.

(5). Why speak of Silvanus and Timothy and himself as the preachers of the Christ just described? 19.

As a fitting contrast to the judaizing preachers of a partial Christ in whom there would be an inconsistent combination of "yea and nay" respecting the promises.

¶ IV. *Statement of His Real Motives in Changing His Plan of Visitation and Further Instructions Touching the Now Penitent Offender Whose Conduct Mainly Had Led to This Change. i. 23–ii. 11.*

1. Strong assertion of the true reason for the change in his plans=But I call God for a witness upon my soul, that to spare you I forbare to come unto Corinth. 23.

2. Anticipated false construction of this statement obviated =(A) Not that we have lordship over your faith, (B) but are helpers of your joy: 24.

3. Ground of this disclaimer of lordship=for by faith you stand.

4. Additional ground of delay as to his visit=But (A) I determined this for myself, (B) that I would not come again to you with sorrow. ii. 1.

5. Expansion of this thought=For (A) if I make you sorry, (B) who then is he that makes me glad, (B²) but he that is made sorry by me? 2.

6. His object in previously communicating this to them= And I wrote this very thing, lest, (A) when I came, (B) I should have sorrow from those of whom I ought to rejoice; 3.

7. Final cause of this step=having confidence in you all, that my joy is the joy of you all.

8. This evinced by the spirit in which he wrote=For I wrote unto you with many tears; (A) out of much affliction (B) and anguish of heart 4.

9. End in view=(A) not that you should be made sorry, (B) but that you might know the love which I have more abundantly unto you.

10. Original source and bearings of the sorrow in the case =But if any has caused sorrow, (A) he has caused sorrow, not to me, (B) but to you all (a) in part (b) (that I press not too heavily). 5.

11. Decision as to the punishment received by the offender =Sufficient to such a one is this punishment which was inflicted by the many ; 6.

12. Consequent duty in the case=so that contrariwise you (A) should rather forgive him, (B) and comfort him, 7.

13. A good end to be thus gained=lest by any means such a one should be swallowed up with his overmuch sorrow.

14. Consequent exhortation=Wherefore I beseech you to confirm your love toward him. 8.

15. This duty had in view in his previous instruction=For to this end (A) also did I write, (B) that I might know the proof of you, (B²) whether you are obedient in all things. 9.

16. Association of himself with the Corinthians in the discharge of this duty=But (A) to whom you forgive anything, (B) I forgive also : 10.

17. Ground of this association=For what I also have forgiven, (A) if I have forgiven anything, (B) for your sakes have I forgiven it in the person of Christ :

18. A great evil to be thus avoided=that no advantage may be gained over us by Satan : 11.

19. Ground of apprehension in the case=For we are not ignorant of his devices.

Queries.

(1). What reasons for thinking the offender here mentioned to be the incestuous man of I. Cor. v. 1–8? 6, 7.

(a). The enormity of his guilt made that offender the most conspicuous sinner in the church at Corinth. (b). He was the only one singled out individually for special animadversion. (c). From no other was the congregation peremptorily commanded to withdraw fellowship. All of these considerations are presupposed in the paragraph before us.

(2). What light is thus thrown on I. Cor. v. 5?

It is seen that the deliverance to Satan there commanded is the withdrawal of fellowship here recognized. And that "the destruction of the flesh" to which reference is there made is its crucifixion through penitence resulting in restoration.

(3). How the offender represented as punished "by the many"?

Further disclosures in this Epistle will show that some in the Corinthian church—a minority—persisted in opposing the apostle and in disregarding his instructions.

¶ V. *His Feelings toward the Corinthians Further Illustrated by His Extreme Anxiety before Meeting with Titus and His Great Joy on Learning through Him of Their Spiritual Improvement. ii. 12–17.*

1. Reference to his mental unrest=Now I had no relief for my spirit, (A) when I came to Troas for the gospel of Christ, (B) and when a door was opened unto me in the Lord, 12, 13.

2. Reason=because I found not Titus my brother : 13.

3. The consequence=but (A) taking my leave of them, (B) I went forth into Macedonia.

4. Gratitude expressed for the resulting relief=But thanks be unto God, 14.

5. Source of his joy in the case=(A) who always leads us in triumph in Christ, (B) and makes manifest through us the savour of his knowledge in every place.

6. Expansion of this thought=For we are a sweet savour of Christ unto God, (A) in those who are being saved, (B) and in those who are perishing; (B²) to the one a savour from death unto death ; (A²) to the other a savour from life unto life. 15, 16.

7. His qualification for diffusing this "savour" came only from God=And who is sufficient for these things?

8. Consequent contrast between him and the judaizers= For (A) we are not as the many, corrupting the word of God : (B) but in the sight of God speak we in Christ, (a) as of sincerity, (b) as of God. 17.

Queries.

(1). Force of the figure in the use of the term "savour"? 14.

Notice its connection with the triumphal procession to which reference is made in this passage. To the point is the terse but clear statement of Meyer. "How does Paul come upon this image? Through the conception of a *triumph*; for such an event took place amid *perfumes of incense.*"

(2). How to some "a savour from death unto death," and to others "a savour from life unto life"? 16.

We have only to conceive of the twofold figure here used as extended and carry it out in spiritual application. In the perfumed atmosphere of a triumphal procession were the defeated as well as the victorious. To the former the fragrance was a token of present ruin and prospective death, but to the latter the token of present triumph and future safety. So all those who find in "the savour" of divine "knowledge" only an atmosphere of unbelief have "been judged already," (Jno. iii. 18) and are in the way to further condemnation, while those who accept this divine "savour" as the "power of God unto salvation" are now alive "unto God" and are in the way to eternal life.

¶ VI. *Contrast between the "Ministration of Righteousness" in the Hands of Paul and the "Ministration of Condemnation" Enforced by His Judaizing Opponents. iii. 1–11.*

1. A false construction of what he had said of himself repudiated=Are we beginning again to commend ourselves? 1.

2. Consequent denial of any need to resort to the practice of his opponents=Or need we, as do some, (A) epistles of commendation to you (B) or from you?

3. Proof of his exemption from such necessity=You are our epistle, (A) written in our hearts, (B) known and read of all men ; 2.

4. The proof more fully developed=being made manifest that you are an epistle of Christ, (A) ministered by us, (B) written (a) not with ink, (b) but with the Spirit of the living God ; (a²) not in tables of stone, (b²) but in tables that are hearts of flesh. 3.

5. Divine support of this assurance=and such confidence have we through Christ to God-ward : 4.

6. Consequent reliance on the true source of ministerial power=(A) not that we are sufficient of ourselves, (A²) to account anything as from ourselves ; (B) but our sufficiency is from God ; 5.

7. Doctrinal ground of this competency=who also made us sufficient (A) as ministers of a new covenant ; (B) not of the letter, (A²) but of the spirit : 6.

8. This justified by the radical difference between the effects of the two covenants=(A) for the letter kills, (B) but the spirit gives life.

9. Justified also by difference of excellence=(A) But if the ministration of death, written and engraven on stones, came with glory, (a) so that the children of Israel could not look stedfastly upon the face of Moses (a²) for the glory of his face ; (b) which glory was

passing away : (B) how shall not rather the ministration of the spirit be with glory? 7, 8.

10. This difference of excellence grounded on a difference of nature=(A) For if the ministration of condemnation is glory, (B) much rather does the ministration of righteousness exceed in glory. 9.

11. Consequent disappearance of the old covenant glory by comparison with the higher glory of the new=For verily that which has been made glorious (A) has not been made glorious in this respect, (B) by reason of the glory that surpasses. 10.

12. Additional ground of superior glory in the new covenant=For (A) if that which passes away was with glory, (B) much more that which remains is in glory. 11.

Queries.

(1). Our analysis identifies "the letter" that "kills" with the old covenant and "the spirit" that "gives life" with the new. What ground for this? 6.

It is evident that the contrast introduced here is continued in ver. 7, 8 and the description given in these verses settles the question. "If the ministration of death, written, and engraven on stones, came with glory, * * * how shall not rather the ministration of the spirit be with glory?" The legal covenant as "written, and engraven on stones" is "the letter" and as it is "the ministration of death" it is rightly described as "the letter" that "kills." By contrast "the ministration of the spirit," previously called "the spirit" that "gives life" is the "new covenant" mentioned in ver. 6 of which the apostle says that he and his apostolic associates were "sufficient as ministers." To suppose, as did Origen, that the contrast of ver. 6 between "the letter" and "the spirit" is a contrast between the literal sense of Scripture and some mystical meaning ; or to suppose with many of our time that it is a contrast between the written word itself and the Holy Spirit that gave it ; or even to suppose, as do some, that it is a contrast between the legalistic spirit of the old dispensation and the gracious spirit of the new, is to utterly ignore the context and the simple connection of thought with thought in the clear reasoning of the apostle.

(2). Why should the old covenant be described as "the ministration of death," and the new covenant as "the ministration of righteousness" that "gives life"?

Here again the exegetes in general are at sea.   To say with Waite,* for example, that "the old was a dispensation of external law, making exactions, but communicating no inward power of obedience," and that "the spirit which was received through the new, was a life-giving spirit," is to get up a contrast other than the one before Paul's mind and give, besides an erroneous representation.   If the old system was so destitute of moral motive influence that it could "communicate no inward power of obedience," how could David say : "The law of the Lord is perfect, restoring the soul"?   No, the contrast of the passage before us is not touched by any difference between "external exaction" and "inward" spiritual power, but consists in the *utter insufficiency* of the old covenant, and the *all-sufficiency* of the new, to provide salvation for sinful men.   Place men with all their imperfections under a mere legal system embracing those high moral demands that reflect the infinite perfections of God himself, and what must be the result?   Condemnation.   For "it is written, Cursed is every one who continues not in all things that are written in the book of the law, to do them." Gal. iii. 10.   Hence, Paul could say, Rom. vii. 9, "I was alive apart from the law once : but when the commandment came, sin revived, *and I died.*"   It is thus that "the letter kills."   And on the other hand, the gospel does not "give life," in the sene here intended, by "communicating" some "inward power of obedience," but by bringing to poor sinners *those rich provisions of grace in Christ* by which they are saved from the guilt and consequences of transgression.   Those who were accepted under the old dispensation had to await this before they could be "perfected" for Heaven.   *Cf.* Heb. ix. 15 ; xi. 39, 40.

(3).   As the covenant that was "written, and engraven on stones" contained, for the most part, great moral principles that must abide for ever, how can it be said   that it "passes away"?   11. *Cf.* Gal. iii. 13.

As "*the ministration of condemnation*" involving a "curse" from which "Christ redeemed us" it has passed away for ever for all who are "in Christ," and this is the point of view in which the old covenant is considered in the passage before us.   But in so far as it embodies imperishable moral principles, like the irrevocable law of veracity, the law of righteous dealing, the law of holy living, it can never pass away.

¶ VII. *The Contrast between the Two Covenants Continued Evincing the Clearness and Sufficiency of Divine Knowledge through Christ. iii. 12–18.*

1. Nature of contrast indicated=Having therefore such a hope, (A) we use great plainness of speech, (B) and are not as Moses, (a) who put a veil upon his face, (b) that the children of Israel should not look stedfastly on the end of that which was passing away : 12, 13.

2. Symbolic import of this=but their minds were blinded : 14.

3. Practical proof of this fact=for (A) until this very day at the reading of the old covenant the same veil remains unlifted ; (B) which veil is done away in Christ. (A²) But unto this day, whensoever Moses is read, a veil lies upon their hearts. (B²) But whensoever it shall turn to the Lord, the veil is taken away. 14–16.

4. This turning to the Lord identical with turning to the new covenant as the spirit that "gives life"=Now the Lord is "the Spirit :" 17.

5. Consequence of this turning to the Spirit that "gives life" =and where the Spirit of the Lord is, there is liberty.

6. Additional result=But we all, with unveiled face reflecting as a mirror the glory of the Lord, (A) are transformed into the same image from glory to glory, (B) even as from the Lord the Spirit. 18.

Queries.

(1). Reference in the word "hope" of verse 12? See 4, 6, 11.

(2). Justify the retention of "plainness" and "blindness" in verses 12–14. Note the point of contrast.

(3). Explain the symbolic import of the veiling of Moses. 13.

As the face of Moses was covered by a veil, so the true significance of the covenant given through him was unperceived by them. The veil of obscurity was upon their heart. And "until this very day at the reading of the old covenant remains the same veil unlifted ;" 14.

(4). How the veil "taken away" in the turning of the heart to the Lord? 16. *Cf.* Luke xxiv. 44–47 ; Acts viii. 34–39. The idea that this veil signifies human depravity, under the influence of which the light of divine truth is shut out of the mind, and that this obstruction is removed by a miraculous turning of the heart to God is absolutely foreign to the subject in hand and the entire treatment of it by the apostle. It was not moral turpitude but mental blindness that prevented the Jews from comprehending the real significance and transitory nature of the legal system. Nor could they possibly understand the shadows of the old dispensation without turning to the spiritual realities of the new as presenting at once the fulfilment and explanation of the typical and temporary institutions of Moses.

(5). Justify the view which the analysis gives of the statement, "the Lord is the Spirit." 17.

It is especially at this point in the paragraph that expositors seem forgetful of the subject in hand and of the clear indications of the context. The clear-headed Kling, generally so satisfactory in his comments, says : "we find here such an identification of Christ and the Holy Spirit, that the Lord, to whom the heart turns, is in no practical respect different from the Holy Spirit received in conversion." Substantially the same exposition is given by Alford, Meyer, Waite, and others. Now if Christ could with any propriety under any point of view be identified with the Holy Spirit, there is certainly no call for such identification in this paragraph. We have here throughout a broad contrast between two covenants called respectively in ver. 6 "the letter" and "the spirit," the one proceeding from the veiled Moses at Sinai ; the other emanating from the unveiled Christ on Mt. Zion. In the expression, ver 15, "whensoever Moses *is read*," it is clear that "Moses" stands by Metonymy for "the letter" or legal covenant which Moses gave, and by force of contrast "the Lord" in ver. 17, stands in the same way for "the spirit," or gracious covenant of which he is the author. Fully stated the whole antithesis would stand thus : Now Moses is "the letter" and where "the letter" of Moses is there is bondage, Gal. iv. 24, 25 ; but "the Lord is the Spirit : and where the Spirit of the Lord is, there is liberty." *Cf.* Gal. v. 1. And what a telling argument against the Judaizers who are here in view !

¶ VIII.   *Vindication of His Apostolic Ministry in the Light
of the Foregoing Contrasts. iv. 1–6.*

1.   Influence of his ministry on himself==Therefore seeing we
have this ministry, (A) even as we obtained mercy, (B) we faint
not : 1.

2.   Practical consequence==but we have renounced the hidden
things of shame, (A) not walking in craftiness, (A²) nor handling
the word of God deceitfully ; (B) but by the manifestation of the
truth commending ourselves (a) to every man's conscience (b) in
the sight of God. 2.

3.   Designation of the only class impervious to the clear light
of this gospel==But and if our gospel is veiled, it is veiled to those
who are perishing : 3.

4.   Explanation of their darkened condition==in whom the
god of this world (A) has blinded the minds of the unbelieving,
(B) that the light of the gospel of the glory of Christ, who is the
image of God, should not dawn upon them. 4.

5.   Reason for calling this "the gospel of the glory of
Christ"==For (A) we preach not ourselves, (B) but Christ Jesus
as Lord, (A²) and ourselves (a) as your servants (b) for Jesus' sake.
5.

6.   Original source of its glorious light==Seeing it is God, (A)
that said, Light shall shine out of darkness, (B) who shined in
our hearts, (B²) to give the light of the knowledge of the glory
of God in the face of Jesus Christ. 6.

Queries.

(1).   What "the hidden things of shame" condemned by
Paul? 2.

The connection shows that reference is not here made to
moral pollution but to the low craftiness which through shame
the Judaizers concealed.

(2).   How unbelievers blinded by "the god of this world"?
4.

Even if reference is here made to Satan as the blinding
agent, it is through wordly influences that this blinding is effected.
It is probable, indeed, that we have here "the genitive of appo-
sition" setting forth this world as a god which as absorbing the
attention of men is in all forms of worldliness exceedingly blinding in its influence. *Cf.* the use of the word "god" in Philippians
iii. 19.

(3). What is here implied as to the adaptation of the truth to the human understanding when not thus blinded by external causes? 4.

(4). What the two beautiful analogies in ver. 6?

(5). What shining into the heart to which reference is made in this passage? 6. The whole connection in ver. 1–7 shows that Paul is speaking of the apostolic ministry sustained through the supernatural shining of truth into the hearts of the inspired apostles ; and through the gospel preached by them the divine light "dawned upon" others not blinded by the world.

¶ IX. *The Might of Divine Energy Combined with the Weakness of Human Instrumentality in Carrying Forward This Ministry. iv. 7–18.*

1. The gospel committed to men=But we have this treasure in earthen vessels, 7.

2. Purpose=that the exceeding greatness of the power (A) may be of God, (B) and not from ourselves ;

3. Antithetical illustration=(A) we are pressed on every side, yet not straitened ; (B) perplexed, yet not unto despair ; (C) pursued, yet not forsaken ; (D) smitten down, yet not destroyed ; 8, 9.

4. Antithetical summary of these experiences on the side of distress and that of support=(A) always bearing about in the body the dying of Jesus, (B) that the life also of Jesus may be manifested in our body. (A²) For we who live are alway delivered unto death for Jesus' sake, (B²) that the life also of Jesus may be manifested in our mortal flesh. 10, 11.

5. The benefit thus accruing to the Corinthians=So then (A) death works in us, (B) but life in you. 12.

6. The principle on which this is realized=But (A) having the same spirit of faith, (A²) according to that which is written, (a) I believed, (b) and therefore did I speak ; (B) we (a) also believe, (b) and therefore also we speak ; 13.

7. Ground of this trust=knowing that he who raised up the Lord Jesus (A) shall raise up us also with Jesus, (B) and shall present us with you. 14.

8. Justification of this hope respecting the Corinthians=
For all things are for your sakes, 15.

9. Important result=that the grace, being multiplied through
the many, may cause the thanksgiving to abound unto the glory
of God.

10. Practical consequence of the principles now developed
=Wherefore we faint not; (A) but though our outward man is
decaying, (B) yet our inward man is renewed day by day. 16.

11. Relation of the hardships just described to this result=
For our light affliction, which is for the moment, works for us
more and more exceedingly an eternal weight of glory; 17.

12. A condition=while (A) we look not at the things which
are seen, (B) but at the things which are not seen : 18.

13. Justification of this=for (A) the things which are seen
are temporal; (B) but the things which are not seen are eternal.

Queries.

(1). What figure in the expression "earthen vessels" and
what its force? 7.

Two thoughts are here metaphorically presented. The saving "treasure" was not conveyed to mankind apart from, but *in*,
the ministerial vessels chosen for that purpose by the Lord. *Cf.*
Acts ix. 15. But while *in* them this divine treasure was not *of*
them since they were but "earthen vessels," or human instruments
divinely employed.

(2). How "alway delivered unto death"? 11. Compare I.
Cor. xv. 31.

(3). What "the same spirit of faith" in ver. 13?

The same resolute heart sustained by faith to speak the truth
of Christ in the face of danger that characterized God's ancient
witnesses for the truth under similar circumstances "according
to that which is written." *Cf.* Ps. cxvi. 10.

(4). What variety of antithesis and what the antithetical
points in ver. 17?

We have the triple antithesis. *"Affliction"* now, in contrast
with *"glory"* hereafter; *"light* affliction," versus *"weight* of
glory;" affliction *"for the moment,"* versus *"eternal* weight of
glory."

•   (5).   How look "at the things which are not seen"? 18. See
Heb. xi, 1.

¶ X. *More Specific Indication of the Unseen Eternal Realities
as Standing in Contrast with the Perishable Things of This Life.
v. 1–10.*

1.   Justification of the distinctions drawn in concluding the
preceding paragraph=For we know (A) that if the earthly house
of our tabernacle be dissolved, (B) we have a building from God,
(B²) a house (a) not made with hands, (b) eternal, (c) in the heavens. 1.

2.   Necessity for this exchange=For verily in this we groan,
(A) longing to be clothed upon with our habitation which is from
heaven : (B) if so be that being clothed we shall not be found
naked. 2, 3.

3.   Re-assertion of this necessity=For indeed we who are in
this tabernacle (A) do groan, (B) being burdened ; 4.

4.   Form of the exchange that is desired=(A) not for that
we would be unclothed, (B) but that we would be clothed upon,
(B²) that what is mortal may be swallowed up of life.

5.   The desire here expressed justified by the divine purpose
in the case=Now (A) he that has wrought us for this very thing
is God, (B) who gave unto us the earnest of the Spirit. 5.

6.   Consequent practical effect=(A) Being therefore always
of good courage, (B) and knowing that, (a) whilst we are at home
in the body, (b) we are absent from the Lord ((a²) for we walk
by faith, (b²) not by sight) ; (A²) we are of good courage, I say,
(a) and are willing rather to be absent from the body, (b) and to
be at home with the Lord. 6–8.

7.   Additional result=Wherefore also we make it our aim,
whether at home or absent, to be well-pleasing unto him. 9.

8.   A solemn fact presented as a motive inducing this result
=For (A) we must all be made manifest before the judgment-seat
of Christ ; (B) that each one may receive the things done in the
body, (B²) according to what he has done, (a) whether it be good
(b) or bad. 10.

Queries.

(1). Import of the expression, "earthly house of our tabernacle"? 1.

A Hebraistic form of speech equivalent to "our tabernacle-house upon earth," a mere transitory tent-dwelling for present sojourning in contrast with the imperishable house to be divinely given for eternal habitation.

(2). How this eternal house, or glorified body, represented as "in the heavens"?

As standing in contrast with the earthiness of the natural body the phrase indicates the heavenly mold and proper sphere of the future spiritual body. It does not *now* exist "in the heavens," but, according to I. Cor. xv. 44–46, will be constructed for the saints at the time of the general resurrection.

(3). How "clothed upon with our habitation"? 2. *Cf.* I. Cor. xv. 53–55.

(4). What the antithesis of faith and sight in verse 7? See context.

(5). What refutation of materialism in verse 8?

(6). What idea conveyed as to the state after death?

¶ XI. *Further Account of the Apostle's Ministry Setting Forth the Purity of His Motives and the Blessed Results at Which He Aimed. v. 11–21.*

1. Ground on which he would evince his integrity=Knowing therefore the fear of the Lord, we persuade men, 11.

2. His confidence as to God's approval and that of true men =(A) But we are made manifest unto God; (B) and I hope that we are made manifest also in your consciences.

3. His real object in asserting this claim=(A) We are not again commending ourselves unto you, (B) but speak as giving you occasion of glorying on our behalf, 12.

4. Ulterior end in view=that you may have wherewith to answer those (A) who glory in appearance, (B) and not in heart.

5. Ground of this "answer"=For (A) whether we are beside ourselves, it is unto God; (B) or whether we are of sober mind, it is unto you. 13.

6. Source of this ministerial devotion=For the love of Christ constrains us; 14.

7. This explained=Because we thus judge (A) that one died for all, therefore all died; (B) and he died for all, that they who live (a) should no longer live unto themselves, (b) but unto him who for their sakes died and rose again. 15.

8. Practical consequence=(A) Wherefore we henceforth know no man after the flesh: (B) even though we have known Christ after the flesh, yet now we know him so no more. 16.

9. Logical conclusion from this course of reasoning=Wherefore if any man is in Christ, (A) he is a new creature: (B) the old things are passed away; (A²) behold, they are become new. 17.

10. Divine source of this newness=But all things are of God, 18.

11. Consequent grace toward himself and his fellow-apostles =(A) who reconciled us to himself through Christ, (B) and gave unto us the ministry of reconciliation;

12. Expansion and explanation of this=to wit, that God was in Christ (A) reconciling the world unto himself, (A²) not reckoning unto them their trespasses, (B) and having committed unto us the word of reconciliation. 19.

13. Consequent apostolic function=(A) We are ambassadors therefore on behalf of Christ, (B) as though God were intreating by us: (A²) we beseech you on behalf of Christ, (B²) be you reconciled to God. 20.

14. The atoning ground of this apostolic "ministry of reconciliation"=(A) Him who knew no sin he made to be sin on our behalf; (B) that we might become the righteousness of God in him. 21.

Queries.

(1). How "made manifest" in the consciences of men? 11.

Paul's integrity of purpose and life was manifest to God and he desired that it should be also in the view of the enlightened consciences of men, and under a reverential "fear of the Lord" in full view of the account to be given before him, he would "persuade men" of this honesty of heart when like some of the Corinthians they were disposed to misjudge him.

(2). Import of the expression "*the love of Christ* constrains us"? 14. *Cf.* ver. 15. See Gal. ii. 20.

(3). How have "all died" through the death of one "for all"? 14.

The comment of Meyer *in loco* is most felicitous : "When Christ died the redeeming death for all (comp. ver. 21), all died in respect of their fleshly life with him. This *objective* matter of fact, which Paul here affirms, has its *subjective* realization in the faith of the individuals, through which they have *entered into* that death-fellowship with Christ *given* through his death for all, so that they have now, by means of baptism, become buried with him (Col. ii. 12). Comp. Rom. vi. 4."

(4). When, according to ver. 17, is the "new creature" fully formed?

It is a very prevalent error to regard a change of heart as constituting the whole of regeneration. It is, indeed, a funda-mental requisite apart from which there can be no new creation. But more is embraced according to the conception of Paul in this and other passages. "If any man is *in Christ*, he is a new creat-ure." A change of position or spiritual relationship must follow a change of disposition.

(5). What is it to be "reconciled to God"? 20.

This also embraces more than it is sometimes represented as doing. To say that "God is already reconciled to sinners and only asks them to be reconciled to him" is to lose sight of the full signifi-cance of this comprehensive term except one element of its mean-ing. That God is ever ready and abundantly willing to receive all who rightly seek him and himself undergoes no change of disposi-tion in effecting a reconciliation is perfectly evident from the teach-ing of his word. "God commends his own love toward us, in that, while we were yet sinners, Christ died for us." But reconcilia-tion goes further and deeper than this. It involves a mutual coming together in the unity of fellowship and peace. And in the context of the very passage just quoted we learn that it is only on being "justified by faith" that we can "have peace with God through our Lord Jesus Christ." Rom. v. 1. And we learn too from this same context that men *received* the "reconciliation" beyond the subjective act of turning in heart toward him who, as infinitely holy, could have no fellowship with them while remaining in their sins.

(6). How Jesus "made to be sin on our behalf"? 21.

If the word sin denotes anywhere "a sin offering," a meaning, indeed, not justified by usage, it certainly has no such significance in this passage. It stands in contrast with "righteousness" on the other side of the antithesis and in both terms we have by Metonymy the abstract for the concrete. Christ was accounted as one sinful and treated as such in bearing *our* guilt that we might be accounted as righteous while standing "in him" before God. The offering of himself for us is implied in the whole statement and not indicated by the word "sin." Moreover, there is a subordinate antithesis in the first clause in which the word "sin" is twice used manifestly in the same sense. It would hardly do to say : "Him who knew no sin offering he made to be a sin offering."

(7). State the full force of the doctrinal antithesis in ver. 21. *Cf.* Rom. viii. 3, 4 ; I. Pet. ii. 24, 25 ; Is. liii. 4–6.

Here again, as in ver. 14 and I. Cor. i. 18–24, we meet with that "doctrine of the cross" which was "a stumblingblock" to legalistic Jews and "foolishness" to worldly-wise Greeks, and which is now no less offensive to egotistic rationalists. In virtue of his relation to the race, the sinless Christ takes the place of sinful man before the divine law and as a consequence of his redemptive work through his atoning death, all who enter into him are clothed with "the righteousness of God in him" through forgiveness. Rom. iv. 6–8 ; Eph. i. 7. No false exegesis can "explain away" this plain teaching of the passage in hand and the parallel Scriptures to which reference is made above. And if the inspired Paul was a blunderer in this cardinal matter, his infallible Lord, the Son of God was no less a blunderer in sending such a teacher to the nations of the earth "to open their eyes, and to turn them from darkness to light, and from the power of Satan unto God."

¶ XII. *Practical Demands and Special Characteristics of His Ministry and the Contrasted Phases of His Ministerial Course.*
vi. 1–10.

1. A ministerial function additional to urging the duty of reconciliation=And working together with him we intreat also that you receive not the grace of God in vain 1.

2. Scriptural ground of this admonition=(for he says, (A)
At an acceptable time I hearkened unto thee, (B) And in a day
of salvation did I succour thee : 2.

3. This Scripture fulfilled under the apostle's ministry=(A)
behold, now is the acceptable time ; (B) behold, now is the day
of salvation) :

4. The admonition enforced by ministerial example=(A)
giving no occasion of stumbling in anything, (A²) that our ministration be not blamed ; (B) but in everything commending ourselves, as ministers of God, 3, 4.

5. Manner of this commendation=in much patience, 4.

6. This explained in detail=(A) in afflictions, in necessities,
in distresses, (B) in stripes, in imprisonments, in tumults, (C) in
labours, in watchings, in fastings ; 4, 5.

7. This commendation further enforced by Christian graces
=(A) in pureness, (B) in knowledge, (C) in longsuffering, (D)
in kindness, (E) in the Holy Spirit, (F) in love unfeigned, (G) in
the word of truth, (H) in the power of God ; 6, 7.

8. Still further enforced by the character of his warfare=
by the armour of righteousness (A) on the right hand (B) and on
the left, 7.

9. Antithetically illustrated by the conflicting estimates of
friends and opponents=(A) by glory and dishonour, (B) by evil
report and good report ; 8.

10. Consequent enumeration of contrasts in the estimation
of his character and life=(A) as deceivers, and yet true ; (B) as
unknown, and yet well known ; (C) as dying, and behold, we live ;
(D) as chastened, and not killed ; (E) as sorrowful, yet alway
rejoicing ; (F) as poor, yet making many rich ; (G) as having
nothing, and yet possessing all things. 8–10.

Queries.

(1). What implied in the admonition to "receive not the
grace of God in vain"? 1. Comp. also II. Pet. i. 10.

(2). How "now the day of salvation"? 2. Comp. John xii.
47, 48.

(3). What forcible figure of speech in 8–10?

¶ XIII. *More Specific Exemplification of the Practical Demands of "the Word of Reconciliation." vi. 11–vii. 1.*

1. Readiness to instruct and exhort in the fulness of apostolic affection=O Corinthians, (A) our mouth is open unto you, (B) our heart is enlarged. 11.

2. Consequent allegation that the lack of enlargement is wholly on their side=(A) Ye are not straitened in us, (B) but ye are straitened in your own affections. 12.

3. A fatherly intreaty for filial requital in this matter=(A) Now for a recompense in like kind (B) (I speak as unto my children), (A²) be ye also enlarged. 13.

4. Resulting exhortation from his enlargement of heart=Be not unequally yoked with unbelievers : 14.

5. Argumentative enforcement of this=(A) for what fellowship have righteousness and iniquity? (B) or what communion has light with darkness? (c) And what concord has Christ with Belial? (D) or what portion has a believer with an unbeliever? (E) And what agreement has a temple of God with idols? 14, 15, 16.

6. Justification of the figure last employed=for we are a temple of the living God ; 16.

7. Scriptural confirmation=even as God said, (A) I will dwell in them, (A²) and walk in them ; (B) and will be their God, (c) and they shall be my people.

8. Consequent Scriptural enforcement of the original exhortation=Wherefore, says the Lord, (A) Come ye out from among them, (A²) and be ye separate, (B) And touch no unclean thing ; 17.

9. The divine promise in the case=And, says the Lord Almighty, (A) I will receive you, (B) and will be to you a Father, (B²) And you shall be to me sons and daughters. 18.

10. Hortatory conclusion=Having therefore these promises, beloved, (A) let us cleanse ourselves from all defilement (a) of flesh (b) and spirit, (B) perfecting holiness in the fear of God. vii. 1.

Queries.

(1). How "Be not unequally yoked with unbelievers"? 14.

It is a prohibition of any sort of connection or association with unbelievers that would interfere with the full and faithful discharge of Christian duty.

(2). How cleanse from "defilement of flesh and spirit"? vii. 1. *Cf*. Matt. xxiii. 25, 26.

The Scriptures abundantly show that outward decency is nothing in the sight of God apart from inward purity.

(3). What perfection in holiness attainable? vii. 1.

According to I. Jno. i. 8, there is no absolute freedom from moral imperfection in this life. Hence, perfection in holiness can be affirmed only in a relative sense of even the most spiritually advanced Christian.

¶ XIV. *The Apostle's Joy over the Reformation of the Corinthians Effected through His Previous Instructions and Admonitions. vii. 2–16.*

1. Repeated request for enlargement of heart toward him= Open your hearts to us: 2.

2. Ground of the request=(A) we wronged no man, (B) we corrupted no man, (C) we took advantage of no man.

3. Misconception obviated=I say it not to condemn you: 3.

4. Proof that such was not his aim=for I have said before, that you are in our hearts (A) to die together (B) and live together.

5. Additional evidence=(A) Great is my boldness of speech toward you, (B) great is my glorying on your behalf: (C) I am filled with comfort, (D) I overflow with joy in all our affliction. 4.

6. Specification of the tribulation that called for comfort= For even when we were come into Macedonia, (A) our flesh had no relief, (B) but we were afflicted on every side; (a)without were fightings, (b) within were fears. 5.

7. Source and manner of the comfort=Nevertheless (A) he that comforts the lowly, even God, (B) comforted us by the coming of Titus; 6.

8. Way in which the comfort was increased=(A) and not by his coming only, (B) but also by the comfort wherewith he was comforted in you, (B²) while he told us your longing, your mourning, your zeal for me; 7.

9. Consequent increase of the apostle's joy=so that I rejoiced yet more.

10. The joy thus resulting a justification of previous warnings=For (A) though I made you sorry with my epistle, (a) I do

not regret it, (b) though I did regret; (B) for I see that that epistle (a) made you sorry, (b) though but for a season. 8.

11. Fuller statement of the ground of his joy=Now I rejoice, (A) not that you were made sorry, (B) but that you were made sorry unto repentance: 9.

12. Explanatory reason=for (A) you were made sorry after a godly sort, (B) that you might suffer loss by us in nothing.

13. This contrast of gain and loss more fully set forth=For (A) godly sorrow works repentance unto salvation, (A^2) a repentance which brings no regret: (B) but the sorrow of the world works death. 10.

14. The productive influence of godly sorrow exhibited by an analysis of the repentance thus wrought in the Corinthians= For behold, this selfsame thing, that you were made sorry after a godly sort, (A) what earnest care it wrought in you, (B) yea, what clearing of yourselves, (C) yea, what indignation, (D) yea, what fear, (E) yea, what longing, (F) yea, what zeal, (G) yea, what avenging! 11.

15. General result of this process=In everything you approved yourselves to be pure in the matter.

16. Consequent re-assertion of his motive in previously writing to them=So although I wrote unto you, (A) I wrote not for his cause that did the wrong, (A^2) nor for his cause that suffered the wrong, (B) but that your earnest care for us might be made manifest unto you in the sight of God. 12.

17. Statement of results=(A) Therefore we have been comforted: (B) and in our comfort we joyed the more exceedingly for the joy of Titus, 13.

18. Re-statement of the ground of joy on the part of Titus =because his spirit has been refreshed by you all.

19. Consequent justification of his confidence in the Corinthians=For if in anything I have gloried to him on your behalf, (A) I was not put to shame; (B) but as we spake all things to you in truth, (B^2) so our glorying also, which I made before Titus, was found to be truth. 14.

20. Resulting effect upon Titus=(A) And his inward affection is more abundantly toward you, (B) whilst he remembers the obedience of you all, (B^2) how with fear and trembling you received him. 15.

21.   Concluding expression of his abiding confidence in the case=I rejoice that in everything I am of good courage concerning you. 16.

Queries.

(1).   The apostle "did regret" what? ver. 8.

Certainly not the writing of the Epistle alluded to—the First to the Corinthians—for the value of the instruction therein to the church of Christ at large would preclude such regret; and, besides, we cannot suppose that the production of such important writings by inspired men was simply left to their own option.   What he regretted was the infliction of pain which he was under the necessity of giving by severe though needed rebukes.   He now rejoices in the beneficial result.

(2).   How "made sorry after a godly sort"? ver. 9.

As standing in contrast with "the sorrow of the world," which is not godly, the phrase evidently denotes the realization of sorrow for a sinful course on account of its opposition to the will and the character of God and not through any mere worldly motive.   Such sorrow for wrong doing reaches the conscience and effects a moral revolution.

(3).   How thus "made sorry" *that* they "might suffer loss" in nothing by the apostle?

Here again, as in many other cases, the connecting conjunction indicates *result* rather than design.   Had Paul neglected the unpleasant duty of reproof and warning they would have "suffered loss" through impenitence.   On the other hand, the result of his faithful dealing with them was the prevention of this "loss" through the earnest reformation effected.   Meyer and Alford, persisting in the advocacy of the theory that the conjunction (hina="that") always denotes purpose, are constrained to refer here and elsewhere to a supposed eternal divine purpose in the case that is manifestly foreign to the thought of the apostle.   Even the Calvinistic Edward Robinson, in his lexicon says, that "this is to introduce a new element of interpretation, and destroy the force of language."

(4).   How this "godly sorrow" related to repentance? *Cf.* ver. 9, 10.

(5).   What, according to the next verse, did the "repentance" of the Corinthians thus produced embrace? 11.

Having said in general terms that "godly sorrow works repentance," the apostle proceeds to specify in detail the several practical elements of the repentance which this sorrow had wrought, or *worked out*, in their case. "Behold, this selfsame thing, that you were made sorry after a godly sort, what *earnest care it wrought* in you, yea, what *clearing of yourselves*, * * yea, what zeal, yea, what avenging! In everything you approved yourselves to be pure in the matter." Repentance therefore, was the whole moral turning in volition and action from the sinful association rebuked by the apostle. It may include more or less of this process on this or that occasion through the force of circumstances not extending in some cases beyond a change of mind or will according to the etymological meaning of the word. It furnishes, indeed, a conspicuous example for the exercise of the caution given by Ernesti in saying that "great care is necessary in the interpreter to guard against rash etymological exegesis, which is often very fallacious." How much more comprehensive than the etymological sense, for instance, is the use of the term when it is said of Jesus that "repentance and remission of sins should be preached in his name unto all the nations"? Two all-important changes are contemplated here : first, *the moral renovation* of man. expressed by repentance, and second, his *entrance into a new spiritual state* in which through forgiveness he enjoys communion with God.

(6). What "the sorrow of the world," and how does such sorrow "work" only "death"? ver. 10

It is not apparent that those exegetes are right, including some of the ablest, who think that we have here the genitive of the subject, denoting the world's sorrow. The contrast between the two kinds of "sorrow" here placed in antithesis would rather indicate the genitive of quality, as in Matt. xiii. 22. As the one kind of sorrow was *godly*, having regard to God in its nature, reaching the conscience in its effect, and resulting finally in salvation, the other sort was simply *worldly* in character kindling only resentment and exasperation under exposure and rebuke, and so leading on to final condemnation.

SECTION SECOND.

CONCERNING A COLLECTION FOR THE POOR SAINTS IN JUDÆA.
viii. 1–ix. 15.

¶ I. *Enforcement of This Duty of Benevolence by the Example of the Macedonians and by the Zeal of the Corinthians in Other Christian Graces. viii. 1–15.*

1. Reference to Macedonian beneficence=Moreover, brethren, we make known to you the grace of God which has been given in the churches of Macedonia ; 1.

2. Manner of its manifestation=how that in much proof of affliction the abundance of their joy and their deep poverty abounded unto the riches of their liberality. 2.

3. Explanatory expansion of this=For (A) according to their power, I bear witness, yea and beyond their power, (B) they gave of their own accord, (c) beseeching us with much intreaty (a) in regard of this grace (b) and the fellowship in the ministering to the saints : 3, 4.

4. Still higher excellence indicated=and this, (A) not as we hoped, (B) but first they gave their own selves (a) to the Lord, (b) and to us by the will of God. 5.

5. Imitation of this example urged=Insomuch that we exhorted Titus, (A) that as he had made a beginning before, (B) so he would also complete in you this grace also. 6.

6. This charity further enforced by the forwardness of the Corinthians in other Christian graces=But (A) as ye abound in everything, (a) in faith, (b) and utterance, (c) and knowledge, (d) and in all earnestness, (e) and in your love to us, (B) see that you abound in this grace also. 7.

7. Nature of his instruction as to this matter= (A) I speak not by way of commandment, (B) but as proving through the earnestness of others the sincerity also of your love. 8.

8. This appeal for a spontaneous beneficence enforced by Christ's example=For ye know the grace of our Lord Jesus Christ, (A) that, though he was rich, (B) yet for your sakes (a) he became poor, (b) that ye through his poverty might become rich. 9.

9. Consequent giving of advice in preference to precept= (A) And herein I give my judgment : (B) for this is expedient for you, 10.

10. Justified by a historic fact in their case=who were the
first to make a beginning a year ago, (A) not only to do, (B) but
also to will.

11. Consequent exhortation to a fulfilment of their purpose
=But now (A) complete the doing also; (B) that as there was
the readiness to will, (A²) so there may be the completion also out
of your ability. 11.

12. Explanatory reason=For if the readiness is there, (A) it
is acceptable according as a man has, (B) not according as he has
not. 12.

13. Explanation expanded to obviate misapprehension=(A)
For I say not this, (a) that others may be eased, (b) and you dis-
tressed : (B) but by equality ; (a) your abundance being a supply
at this present time for their want, (b) that their abundance also
may become a supply for your want ; (B²) that there may be equality : 13, 14.

14. Scriptural illustration of this principle of equality=as it
is written, (A) He that gathered much had nothing over ; (B) and
he that gathered little had no lack. 15.

Queries.

(1). What the "grace of God which has been given in the
churches of Macedonia"? 1.

By comparing ver. 2, 4 and 7 it is clear that the direct reference is to the *liberal donation made by those churches* for the poor
saints of Judæa. It is not, then, the grace bestowed upon the
Macedonian churches or the grace divinely shed abroad among
them, but the objective grace of liberality flowing from the
churches themselves as moved, of course, by him "who works"
in believers "both to will and to work, for his good pleasure."
The term grace is here used by Metonymy to denote, not the
principle itself, but its practical manifestation in the actual gift.

(2). Distinction of "commandment" and "judgment"? 8,
10. *Cf.* I. Cor. vii. 6.

(3). How "not only to do, but also to will"? 10.
One might naturally ask, does not the doing involve a previous
willing, and why then speak of a beginning "not only to do, but
also to will"? But the context (*Cf.* ver. 12) justifies the order
given by the apostle. In beneficence we must not only act but
couple with the act the willingness and cordiality of love.

"And if I bestow all my goods to feed the poor, and if I give my body to be burned, but have not love it profits me nothing."

(4). What the conditions of "acceptable giving"? 12.

¶ II. *Commendation of Those Who were Engaged in Superintending the Collection. viii. 16–24.*

1. Thanks for the zeal of Titus in the matter==But thanks be to God, who puts the same earnest care for you into the heart of Titus. 16.

2. Justification of this gratitude==For indeed (A) he accepted our exhortation ; (B) but (a) being himself very earnest, (b) he went forth, unto you of his own accord. 17.

3. Complimentary reference to his assistant==And we have sent together with him the brother whose praise in the gospel is spread through all the churches ; 18.

4. Further information concerning him==(A) and not only so, (B) but who was also appointed by the churches (a) to travel with us in the matter of this grace, (a^2) which is ministered by us to the glory of the Lord, (b) and to shew our readiness : 19.

5. Precautionary measure in the case==avoiding this, that any man should blame us in the matter of this bounty which is ministered by us : 20.

6. Ground of this carefulness==for we take thought for things honourable, (A) not only in the sight of the Lord, (B) but also in the sight of men. 21.

7. Description of another companion==And we have sent with them our brother, (A) whom we have many times proved earnest in many things, (B) but now (a) much more earnest, (b) by reason of the great confidence which he has in you. 22.

8. Epitome of recommendation==(A) Whether any inquire about Titus, (a) he is my partner, (b) and my fellow-worker to you-ward ; (B) or our brethren, (a) they are the messengers of the churches, (b) they are the glory of Christ. 23.

9. Consequent intreaty as to the treatment due to them== Shew ye therefore unto them in the face of the churches (A) the proof of your love, (B) and of our glorying on your behalf. 24.

Queries.

(1). Import and importance of the precept "take thought for things honourable" in the sight of men? 21. Comp. also Rom. xii. 17.

(2). How Titus a "partner" of Paul? 23.

¶ III. *Additional Inducements Presented to the Corinthians to Renew Their Original Readiness in This Beneficence by a Prompt Response to Titus and His Companions. ix. 1–15.*

1. Recognition of their willingness to contribute=For as touching the ministering to the saints, it is superfluous for me to write to you : 1.

2. Ground of this recognition=for (A) I know your readiness, (B) of which I glory on your behalf to them of Macedonia, (A²) that Achaia has been prepared for a year past ; 2.

3. Effect of this glorying=and your zeal has stirred up very many of them.

4. The means employed to quicken this willingness=But I have sent the brethren, (A) that our glorying on your behalf may not be made void in this respect ; (B) that, even as I said, you may be prepared : 3.

5. Reason for this precaution=lest by any means, (A) if there come with me any of Macedonia, and find you unprepared, (B) we (that we say not, you) should be put to shame in this confidence. 4.

6. Re-assertion of his purpose in adopting this measure=I thought it necessary therefore to intreat the brethren, (A) that they (a) would go before unto you, (b) and make up beforehand your aforepromised bounty, (B) that the same might be ready, (a) as a matter of bounty, (b) and not of extortion. 5.

7. Argument for bountiful giving=But this I say, (A) He that sows sparingly shall reap also sparingly ; (B) and he that sows bountifully shall reap also bountifully. 6.

8. This to be a heart-felt beneficence=(A) Let each man do according as he has purposed in his heart ; (a) not grudgingly, (b) or of necessity : (B) for God loves a cheerful giver. 7.

9. Argument for this beneficence based on God's power to furnish all means to this end=(A) And God is able to make all

grace abound unto you; (B) that you may abound unto every good work, (A²) having always all sufficiency in everything : 8.

10. Scriptural illustration=as it is written, (A) He has scattered abroad, (A²) he has given to the poor; (B) his righteousness abides for ever. 9.

11. Additional argument from God's willingness as commensurate with his ability in the case=And he that supplies seed to the sower and bread for food, (A) shall supply and multiply your seed for sowing, (B) and increase the fruits of your righteousness. 10 :

12. Consequence=(A) you being enriched in everything unto all liberality, (B) which works through us thanksgiving to God. 11.

13. Explanatory justification of this statement by the twofold end of the charity required=For the ministration of this service (A) not only fills up the measure of the wants of the saints, (B) but abounds also through many thanksgivings unto God : 12.

14. Expansion of this thought=seeing (A) that through the proving of you by this ministration (B) they glorify God (a) for the obedience of your confession unto the gospel of Christ, (b) and for the liberality of your contribution unto them and unto all; 13.

15. Additional result effected=while they themselves also, (A) with supplication on your behalf, (B) long after you by reason of the exceeding grace of God in you. 14.

16. Concluding outburst of gratitude for God's beneficent grace=Thanks be to God for his unspeakable gift. 15.

Queries.

(1). Vindicate the politic course of Paul described in ver. 2-4.

From what he says in ver. 3 and especially in ver. 4, it has been inferred by some that the boast in ver. 2 to the Macedonians of the readiness of Achaia for a year, was unjustifiable and wrongly used for present effect exposing his course in this matter to the charge that it was "not free from human error." We give the following from Meyer as a satisfactory defence of the apostle : "Paul might with perfect truth stimulate (1) the Macedonians by the zeal of the Corinthians, because the latter had begun the work *earlier* than the former and were already a year ago in readiness, and then, (2) the Corinthians, again, by the example of the Macedonians,

since the latter, after having followed the Corinthians in the pros-
ecution of the work, had shown such extraordinary activity as in
turn to serve the Corinthians a model and a stimulus to *further*
beneficence. Is it not possible that in the very same affair first A
should be held up as a model to B, and then, according to the
measure of success, conversely B to A?"

(2). How the contribution sought "as a matter of bounty"?
5. Comp. 6, 7.

(3). What principle of usage illustrated by the employment
of the word "righteousness" in 9 as compared with righteous in
Rom. v. 7?

SECTION THIRD.
RENEWAL OF THE APOSTLE'S DEFENCE OF HIS AUTHORITY
AND EFFICIENCY WITH A VIEW TO AN UNSPARING
EXPOSURE OF HIS IRRECONCILABLE TRADUCERS.
x. 1–xiii. 14.

¶ I. *His Means of Achieving a Conquest over All Adversaries
of the Gospel. x. 1–6.*

1. Motive to enforce intreaty=Now I Paul myself intreat
you by the meekness and gentleness of Christ; 1.

2. The consideration suggestive of this motive=I who (A)
in your presence am lowly among you, (B) but being absent am
of good couarge toward you,

3. Allusion to a misrepresentation of this fact involving a
warning in the case=yea, I beseech you, that I may not when
present shew courage (A) with the confidence wherewith I count
to be bold against some, (B) who count of us as if we walked
according to the flesh. 2.

4. Repudiation of the course of life falsely charged=For
(A) though we walk in the flesh, (B) we do not war according to
the flesh 3.

5. Justification of this statement=(for the weapons of our
warfare (A) are not of the flesh, (B) but mighty before God to
the casting down of strong holds); 4.

6. Expansion and explanation=(A) casting down (a) vain
reasonings (b) and every high thing that is exalted against the

knowledge of God, (ʙ) and bringing every thought into captivity
to the obedience of Christ; 5.

7. Relation of this warfare to the incorrigible=and being
in readiness (ᴀ) to avenge all disobedience, (ʙ) when your
obedience shall be fulfilled. 6.

Queries.

(1). Point in the charge that the apostle "walked according
to the flesh"? 2.

Notice the tenor of his vindication and apply the "Law of
Opposition." It is not probable that any one ever presumed to
charge him with immorality.

(2). What "the knowledge of God" and what "every high
thing" exalted against it? 5.

The whole course of thought shows this knowledge to be the
truth concerning God and his will as revealed in Christ which
Paul defended against both judaizing opponents and philosophic
disputants. In reference to these he had already triumphantly
asked : "Where is the wise? where is the scribe? where is the
disputer of this world? has not God made foolish the wisdom of
the world?" But what was seen then is often repeated in our
own day. The vain reasonings of rationalists, "puffed up" with
the conceit of their own wisdom, are "exalted against" the infallible teaching of the Son of God and his inspired apostles. And
Paul's admonition is not less appropriate now than when it first
came with burning energy from his earnest soul. "Let no man
deceive himself. If any man thinks that he is wise among you
in this world, let him become a fool, that he may become wise."

(3). How "avenge all disobedience"? 6.

When Paul had won back to Christ all who could be brought
from under the seductive influence of his opponents, thus leading
their very thoughts "into captivity to the obedience of Christ,"
he would then be ready to exercise disciplinary power over all
who would persist in disobedience. The figurative representation
is based on military usage in reducing some adversaries to submission and subjecting the rest to punishment.

¶ II. *The Contrast between His Own Course and That of His Opponents. x. 7–18.*

1. The objectors governed by appearances=You look at the things that are before your face. 7.

2. The simple exercise of judgment should convince them of his claims=(a) If any man trusts in himself that he is Christ's, (b) let him consider this again with himself, (a) that, even as he is Christ's, (b) so also are we.

3. Assertion of power to justify his claims=For (a) though I should glory somewhat abundantly concerning our authority ((a) which the Lord gave for building you up, (b) and not for casting you down), (b) I shall not be put to shame : 8.

4. His reason for not threatening its exercise=that I may not seem as if I would terrify you by my letters. 9.

5. Occasion of this reference to his writings=For, (a) His letters, they say, are weighty and strong; (b) but (a) his bodily presence is weak, (b) and his speech of no account. 10.

6. Consequent warning=Let such a one reckon this, (a) that, what we are in word by letters when we are absent, (b) such are we also in deed when we are present. 11.

7. Admission of the lack of the sort of courage his opponents possessed=For we are not bold to number or compare ourselves with certain of those who commend themselves : 12.

8. Explanatory description of this trait in them=but they themselves, measuring themselves by themselves, and comparing themselves with themselves, are without understanding.

9. His own case in contrast=(a) But we will not glory beyond our measure, (b) but according to the measure of the province (a) which God apportioned to us as a measure, (b) to reach even unto you. 13.

10. Explanatory justification of this=For (a) we stretch not ourselves overmuch, (b) as though we reached not unto you : (B^2) for we came even as far as unto you in the gospel of Christ : 14.

11. Repetition and expansion=(a) not glorying beyond our measure, (A^2) that is, in other men's labors; (b) but having hope that, as your faith grows, we shall be magnified in you according to our province unto further abundance, 15..

12. Ultimate aim=so as (a) to preach the gospel even unto the parts beyond you, (b) and not to glory in another's province in regard to things ready to our hand. 16.

13. The Scriptural rule to govern in the matter=But he who glories, let him glory in the Lord. 17.

14. The propriety of this=(A) For not he who commends himself is approved, (B) but whom the Lord commends. 18.

Queries.

(1). How "not be put to shame" for glorying concerning authority bestowed? 8. *Cf.* ver. 11 ; I. Cor. iv. 19-21.

(2). How were opponents "measuring themselves by themselves, and comparing themselves with themselves"? 12.

(3). What the measure of the "province" apportioned to. Paul? 13. *Cf.* Acts xxii. 21 ; xxvi. 17.

¶ III. *Ironical Glorying of the Apostle in His Ministerial Work in Opposition to the Empty Boasting of the Judaizers. xi. 1-15.*

1. Tolerance of glorying requested=(A) Would that you could bear with me in a little foolishness : (B) nay indeed bear with me. 1.

2. Ground of this request=For I am jealous over you with a godly jealousy : 2.

3. This metaphorically justified=for (A) I espoused you to one husband, (B) that I might present you as a pure virgin to Christ.

4. Source of his jealousy in the case=But I fear, lest by any means, (A) as the serpent beguiled Eve in his craftiness, (B) your minds should be corrupted from the simplicity and the purity that is toward Christ. 3.

5. Further justification of his request=For you do well to bear with me, (A) if he who comes preaches another Jesus, whom we did not preach, (B) or if you receive a different spirit, which you did not receive, (C) or a different gospel, which you did not accept. 4.

6. Why his glorying could be excused if that of his opponents is allowable=For I reckon that I am not a whit behind those pre-eminent apostles. 5.

7. Vindication of this claim=(A) But though I be rude in speech, (B) yet am I not in knowledge; (B²) nay, in everything we have made it manifest among all men to you-ward. 6.

8. No exception found in his self-denial for their sakes= Or (A) did I commit a sin (a) in abasing myself (B) that you might be exalted, (B²) because I preached to you the gospel of God for nought? 7.

9. Consequent mode of procedure on arriving at Corinth= (A) I robbed other churches, (A²) taking wages of them (B) that I might minister unto you; 8.

10. Method during his residence=and (A) when I was ·present with you and was in want, (B) I was not a burden on any man; (B²) for the brethren, when they came from Macedonia, supplied the measure of my want; 9.

11. His fixed principle of action in the case=(A) and in everything I kept myself from being burdensome unto you, (B) and so will I keep myself.

12. His resolution to maintain this=(A) As the truth of Christ is in me, (B) no man shall stop me of this glorying in the regions of Achaia. 10.

13. A false motive repudiated=Wherefore? (A) because I love you not? (B) God knows. 11.

14. His real purpose set forth=But what I do, that I will do, (A) that I may cut off occasion from those who desire occasion; (B) that wherein they glory, they may be found even as we. 12.

15. Description of these opposers=(A) For such men are false apostles, (B) deceitful workers, (A²) fashioning themselves into apostles of Christ. 13.

16. The description justified=And no marvel; (A) for even Satan fashions himself into an angel of light. (B) It is no great thing therefore if his ministers also fashion themselves as ministers of righteousness; 14, 15.

17. A fitting consequence=whose end shall be according to their works. 15.

Queries.

(1). Justify the rejection of the supplement "him" and the substitution of "me" against the Revised and other versions. 4.

Notice that the apostle begins the paragraph with the wish that the Corinthians would bear with him in the constrained

"foolishness" of boasting, to which he adds the earnest intreaty :
"Nay indeed bear with me." He gives as a reason for this earnestness, his "godly jealousy," over them which fills him with great
anxiety as to their spiritual welfare. He then in ver. 3, 4 adverts
to the source of his fear of their estrangement from Christ through
the perverse teaching of those who were preaching "another
Jesus" than the crucified and risen Christ whom he himself had
preached to them, and were consequently inculcating "a different
gospel" from that which they had received from him. What,
now, could be more appropriate and more closely connected with
this than to end with the enforcement of the earnest intreaty
which begins this train of thought by saying, "you do well to
bear with me" in my anxious effort to expose every such adver-
sary of the truth and to hold you in stedfast loyalty to the redeeming Christ of my gospel? He had said in full form of expression,
"indeed bear with me," and after presenting his argument in justification of this intreaty repeats it in elliptical form, and according to usage the word to be supplied is the one that is found in
the complete form of expression as already employed. To suppose that Paul after speaking of the false teachers who would
preach "a different gospel" from his, *ironically* says, "you do
well to bear with him," leaving the pronoun "him" to be supplied by the reader, is absurd ; for this would require emphasis
upon the pronoun and hence demand its actual appearance in the
sentence. The simple construction is that Paul after intreating
them to bear with him in his effort to detach them from false
teachers shows from the character of their teaching that the Corinthians would do well to bear with him in his effort and accordingly urges them to do so.

(2). With what "apostles" compared in 5? Comp. 13.

(3). How own to "be rude in speech"? 6. Comp. I. Cor.
ii. 1–5.

(4). How "rob other churches" in ministering to the Corinthians? 8. *Cf.* ver. 9.

The support which he could justly claim as due to him from his
Corinthian converts he waived for sufficient reasons and received
from other churches what was needful to meet his wants. The

Corinthians received the benefit of a ministry that was sustained by the benevolence of others.

¶ IV. *Continuance of Ironical Glorying in a More Extended Comparison with the Judaizers. xi. 16-33.*

1. Significance of his glorying=I say again, (A) Let no man think me foolish ; (B) but if you do, (a) yet as foolish receive me, (b) that I also may glory a little. 16.

2. Explanatory comment=That which I speak, (A) I speak not after the Lord, (B) but as in foolishness, (B^2) in this confidence of glorying. 17.

3. Occasion and character of glorying=Seeing that many glory after the flesh, I will glory also. 18.

4. Reason for expecting their tolerance=For you bear with the foolish gladly, being wise yourselves. 19.

5. Practical illustrative proof=For you bear with a man, (A) if he brings you into bondage, (B) if he devours you, (c) if he takes you captive, (D) if he exalts himself, (E) if he smites you on the face. 20.

6. Additional explanatory statement of his case=(A) I speak by way of disparagement, as though we had been weak. (B) Yet whereinsoever any is bold I am bold also. 21.

7. Cautionary explanation parenthetically inserted=(I speak in foolishness),

8. Comparison with any who are bold as to national traits =(A) Are they Hebrews? so am I. (B) Are they Israelites? so am I. (c) Are they the seed of Abraham? so am I. 22.

9. Comparison as to ministerial dignity=(A) Are they ministers of Christ? (B) I more ; 23.

10. Repeated cautionary explanation in parenthesis=(I speak as one beside himself)

11. Justification of his claim in the ministerial comparison =(A) in labours more abundantly, (B) in prisons more abundantly, (c) in stripes above measure, (D) in deaths oft.

12. Practical illustration through actual sufferings=(A) Of the Jews five times received I forty stripes save one. (B) Thrice was I beaten with rods, (c) once was I stoned, (D) thrice I suffered shipwreck, (E) a night and a day have I been in the deep ; 24, 25.

13. Illustration in exposure to dangers=(A) in journeyings often, (B) in perils of rivers, (C) in perils of robbers, (D) in perils from my countrymen, (E) in perils from the Gentiles, (F) in perils in the city, (G) in perils in the wilderness, (H) in perils in the sea, (I) in perils among false brethren ; 26.

14 Illustration through hardships=(A) in labour and travail, (B) in watchings often, (C) in hunger and thirst, (D) in fastings often, (E) in cold and nakedness. 27.

15. A great source of concern additional to all these=(A) Beside those things that are without, (B) there is that which presses upon me daily, (B²) anxiety for all the churches. 28.

16. Illustrative proof=(A) Who is weak, and I am not weak? (B) who is made to stumble, and I burn not? 29.

17. Consequent reference to his only ground of glorying= If I must needs glory, I will glory of the things that concern my weakness. 30.

18. Solemn avowal of truthfulness as to the record here given=The God and Father of our Lord Jesus, he who is blessed for evermore, knows that I lie not. 31.

19. A historic fact specified in confirmation=In Damascus the governor under Aretas the king (A) guarded the city of the Damascenes, in order to take me: (B) and through a window was I let down in a basket by the wall, (B²) and escaped his hands. 32, 33.

Queries.

(1). What *wisdom* manifested in the "foolishness" of the apostle? 17, 21. *Cf.* Prov. xxvi. 5.

In thus ironically dealing with fools "according to" their folly he the more effectually brought the empty and foolish boasting of his judaizing opponents into deserved contempt.

(2). How "speak not after the Lord" in this matter? 17.

Considered abstractly and apart from justifying circumstances his method would involve self-glorification and hence would be out of harmony with Christian humility, as was actually the case with the course of the judaizers.

(3). What important purposes subserved in the enumeration of his trials and afflictions? 24–27.

Here we can see the fulness of meaning and logical force of the argumentative question in I. Cor. xv. 30, which never has been, and never can be, answered by the infidel. Why stand we "in jeopardy every hour?" And here we see the power of the apostle's life as an unanswerable testimonial for Christ and Christianity. His lofty integrity and absolute trustworthiness as a true witness of Jesus find ample support in his unparalleled career of suffering and stand over in bold and striking contrast with the record of his adversaries who encountered no affliction in their senseless opposition to his ministry.

¶ V. *Reference to His Visions and Revelations as Involving Extraordinary Favor, but of Which He Will Glory only as They Stand Related to His Afflictions and Weakness. xii. 1–13.*

1. His glorying due to circumstances alone=(A) I must needs glory, (B) though it is not expedient ; 1.

2. Ground of its possible justification=but I will come to visions and revelations of the Lord.

3. Illustrative instance=(A) I know a man in Christ, (B) fourteen years ago (caught up) (a) (whether in the body, I know not ; (a²) or whether out of the body, I know not ; (b) God knows), (B) such a one caught up even to the third heaven. 2.

4. Repetition and expansion=(A) And I know such a man ((a) whether in the body, or apart from the body, I know not : (b) God knows), (B) how that he was caught up into Paradise, (c) and heard unspeakable words, (c²) which it is not permitted a man to utter. 3, 4.

5. Propriety of glorying in such exaltation maintained= On behalf of such a one will I glory : 5.

6. The only ground of its justification in the sphere of his own individuality=(A) but on mine own behalf I will not glory, (B) save in my weaknesses.

7. Reason for this limitation of glorying=For if I should desire to glory, (A) I shall not be foolish ; (A²) for I shall speak the truth : (B) but I forbear, (a) lest any man should account of me above that which he sees me to be, (b) or hears from me. 6.

8. Mode of precluding all glorying over his visions and revelations=And by reason of the exceeding greatness of the revelations—wherefore, (A) that I should not be exalted overmuch, (B) there was given to me a thorn in the flesh, (B²) a messenger of Satan to buffet me, (A²) that I should not be exalted overmuch. 7.

9.   Its severity indicated=Concerning this thing (A) I besought the Lord thrice, (B) that it might depart from me. 8.

10.   Ground of the Lord's refusal to remove it=And he has said unto me, (A) My grace is sufficient for thee: (B) for my power is made perfect in weakness. 9.

11.   Logical conclusion setting forth his only ground of glory-ing=Most gladly therefore (A) will I rather glory in my weak-nesses, (B) that the strength of Christ may rest upon me. 9.

12.   Conclusion expanded=Wherefore I take pleasure for Christ's sake, (A) in weaknesses, (B) in injuries, (C) in necessities, (D) in persecutions, (E) in distresses, 10.

13.   Reason in paradox=(A) for when I am weak, (B) then am I strong.

14.   His glorying abstractly considered=I am become fool-ish : 11.

15.   His apology=you compelled me ;

16.   Explanation=(A) for I ought to have been commended of you : (B) for in nothing (a) was I behind those pre-eminent apostles, (b) though I am nothing.

17.   Evidence of this claim=Truly the signs of an apostle were wrought among you in all patience, by signs and wonders and mighty works. 12.

18.   This evinced by their spiritual advantages=(A) For what is there wherein you were made inferior to the rest of the churches, (B) except it be that I myself was not a burden to you? (B^2) forgive me this wrong. 13.

Queries.

(1).   What the "third heaven"? ver. 2.

The Scriptures nowhere present the idea of higher and lower stories in the heavenly home of the saints.   And we can only reach a conclusion on the subject from usage in reference to the term heaven.   In many places the atmospheric region, the home of the birds, is called heaven, as in Mark iv. 4, 32 ; Acts xi. 6. As distinct from this usage it is applied to the regions of the stars, as in Matt. xxiv. 29 ; Mark xiii. 25.   In the third place, it signi-fies the final home of the blest in the presence of God. Heb. ix. 24.   This is doubtless the sense in which the word is here employed.

(2). Import of the term "Paradise"? ver. 4. *Cf.* 2.

This is a generic term denoting any place of delight, and its specific application in any given instance must be determined by the context. In the Septuagint it is applied to the garden of Eden. In Luke xxiii. 43 it is applied to the happy abode of the righteous dead awaiting the perfection in Christ. *Cf.* Heb. xi. 39, 40. Here, as the context shows, it is identical with the "third heaven" of ver. 2. Hence, denotes the final home of the blest.

(3). How hear words "not lawful for a man to utter"? 4.

Not lawful in that they could not be translated into the language of earth, or comprehended by men in this life; as words signifying color cannot be intelligible to one who never had sight.

(4). What the interesting matter as to the "thorn in the flesh"? 7.

The important lesson touching the all-sufficiency of the grace of God which Paul learned by his experience in connection with this trouble, is the chief thought that he would impress upon the reader. To overlook this and to spend hours in trying to determine what the thorn itself was is the manifestation of no little folly.

(5). How this thorn a "messenger of Satan"?

He is the original source of all pain and physical evil and as such may be regarded remotely as the source of this "thorn in the flesh."

(6). What figures of speech employed? 1-13.

¶ VI. *An Earnest and Affectionate Effort to Reclaim Those Who Were Disaffected by the Judaizers. xii. 14-21.*

1. His purpose announced=Behold, (A) this is the third time I am ready to come to you; (B) and I will not be a burden to you: 14.

2. Reason=for I seek not yours, but you:

3. This justified by allusion to his relation to them=for (A) the children ought not to lay up for the parents, (B) but the parents for the children.

4. The spirit that moves him in seeking their interest=(A) And I will most gladly spend (B) and be spent for your souls.

5. Consequent tender appeal=If I love you more abundantly, am I loved the less?

6. Reference to a false construction of his motives=(A) But be it so, (B) I did not myself burden you; (B²) but, being crafty, I caught you with guile. 16.

7. Refutation of the charge=(A) Did I take advantage of you by any of those whom I sent unto you? (B) I exhorted Titus, and I sent the brother with him. (B²) Did Titus take any advantage of you? (C) walked we not by the same Spirit? (D) walked we not in the same steps? 17, 18.

8. Reference of his defence to the proper judge in the case= (A) You think all this time that we are excusing ourselves unto you. (B) In the sight of God speak we in Christ. 19.

9. Its true aim=But all things, beloved, are for your edifying.

10. Ground of his action in thus labouring with them before making his visit=For I fear, lest by any means, when I come, (A) I should find you not such as I would, (B) and should myself be found of you such as you would not; 20.

11. Explanation and expansion=(A) lest by any means there should be strife, jealousy, wraths, factions, backbitings, whisperings, swellings, tumults; (B) lest, when I come again, (a) my God should humble me before you, (b) and I should mourn for many of those who have sinned heretofore, and repented not of the uncleanness and fornication and lasciviousness which they have committed. 20, 21.

Queries.

(1). Why consider the statement "being crafty, I caught you with guile" as expressing a charge against him? 16. *Cf.* 17, 18.

His questions, that immediately follow, clearly show that he repudiates the idea of any resort to craftiness or guile in the case. It is thus, really, a defence against such a charge which had been brought against him. In the use of the words crafty and guile he probably quotes the language of his accusers.

(2). How would Paul be found of them such as they would not? 20. *Cf.* xiii. 2.

As having to use his power in not sparing them through the necessity of treating them with deserved severity.

¶ VII. *Warning of the Severity to Which He May be
Driven through Their Impenitence Combined with
Further Exhortation to Spare Him This
Necessity. xiii. 1–10.*

1. Re-announcement of his proposed visit=This is the third
time I am coming to you. 1.

2. Ground of procedure on his arrival=At the mouth of two
witnesses or three shall every word be established.

3. Emphatic statement of his intention to use apostolic
authority=I have said beforehand, and I do say beforehand, as
when I was present the second time, so now, being absent, to
those who have sinned heretofore and to all the rest, that, if I
come again, I will not spare; 2.

4. Ground of this authoritative claim=(A) seeing that you
seek a proof of Christ that speaks in me; (B) who to you-ward
is not weak, (B^2) but is powerful in you : 3.

5. This justified by his resemblance to Christ both in weakness and in power=(A) for he was crucified through weakness,
(B) yet he lives through the power of God. (A^2) For we also
are weak in him, (B^2) but we shall live with him through the
power of God toward you. 4.

6. Consequent admonition to test their own standing rather
than the power of Christ in him=(A) Try your own selves,
whether you be in the faith; (B) prove your own selves. 5.

7. Rule governing the application of this test=Or know
you not as to your own selves, (A) that Jesus Christ is in you?
(B) unless indeed you be reprobate.

8. His confidence as to its application to himself=But I
hope that you shall know that we are not reprobate. 6.

9. A prayer that they test not his punitive power=Now
we pray God that you do no evil; 7.

10. Purport of this explained=(A) not that we may appear
approved, (B) but that you may do that which is honourable, (A^2)
though we be as reprobate.

11. This feeling justified by the true end of his punitive
power=For (A) we can do nothing against the truth, (B) but for
the truth. 8.

12. And confirmed by his joy over a lack of this power in
case of their amendment=For we rejoice, (A) when we are
weak, (B) and you are strong : 9.

13.   This condition of things the object of his prayers=this we also pray for, even your perfecting.

14.   The object also of his epistolary pleadings=For this cause (A) I write these things while absent, (B) that I may not when present deal sharply, (B²) according to the authority which the Lord gave to me (a) for building up, (b) and not for casting down. 10.

Query.

(1).   Contextual import of the statement "we rejoice when we are weak, and you are strong"? 9.

The idea is that he would rejoice when, on account of their spiritual amendment, he would be powerless to resort to the use of authority.

¶ VIII.   *Conclusion.   xiii. 11–14.*

1.   Closing exhortations=Finally, brethren, (A) rejoice. (B) Be perfected; (C) be comforted; (D) be of the same mind; (E) live in peace : 11.

2.   Consequent blessing=and the God of love and peace shall be with you.

3.   Affectionate salutation enjoined=Salute one another with a holy kiss. 12.

4.   Salutation sent=All the saints salute you. 13.

5.   Benediction=[May there] be with you all, (A) the grace of our Lord Jesus Christ, (B) and the love of God, (C) and the communion of the Holy Spirit. 14.

Queries.

(1).   How salute "with a holy kiss"? 12.

The kiss (men kissing men) was merely the Oriental form. The spirit of the injunction is now carried out in other forms.

(2).   What implied in the form of the benediction? 14.

The equality and coordinate agency of the Holy Spirit, Christ and God.

ANALYSIS

OF

GALATIANS.

SECTION FIRST.

PAUL'S DEFENCE OF HIS APOSTOLIC INDEPENDENCE
AND AUTHORITY.

i. 1–ii. 21.

¶ I. *Apostolic Address and Greeting. i. 1–5.*

1.   The author named and the source of his apostleship indi-
cated=Paul, (A) an apostle ((a) not from men, (b) neither
through man, (B) but (a) through Jesus Christ, (b) and God the
Father, who raised him from the dead), 1.

2.   Reference to others as uniting in sending the Epistle=
and all the brethren who are with me, 2.

3.   The parties addressed=unto the churches of Galatia :

4.   Spiritual benediction=Grace to you and peace (A) from
God the Father, (B) and our Lord Jesus Christ, 3.

5.   Redemptive source in Christ of this grace and peace=
who gave himself for our sins, (A) that he might deliver us out
of this present evil world, (B) according to the will of our God
and Father : 4.

6.   Doxology=to whom be the glory for ever and ever. Amen.
5.

Queries.

(1).   Why emphasize the divine source of his apostleship?
1.

From the subsequent defence of his apostolic dignity and
authority it appears that his judaizing opponents, in order to
destroy the effect of his teaching, represented him as inferior to
the original twelve and was dependent upon them for his knowledge of the truth from which, they alleged, he had deflected in
preaching a free salvation.

(2).   In ascribing his apostolic commission and qualification
to Christ, why refer to his resurrection? 1.

On account of the essential connection between the two. As the resurrection of Christ was the indispensable condition of Paul's apostleship, so the latter was a standing proof unanswerably attesting the reality of the former.

(3). What the redemptive work of Christ as here described, and why referred to in this connection? 4.

The statement that he "died for our sins" is illustrated by the further description of the end thus secured in the expression "that he might deliver us out of this present evil world." Such deliverance was wholly dependent upon the agency of Christ, his atoning death "for our sins." And Paul makes early reference to this in the Epistle whose great object is to show against his legalistic opponents that it is here only and not on the basis of law that mankind can find hope of eternal life.

(4). Why speak of this redeeming work of Christ as "according to the will of our God"? 4. *Cf.* Acts ii. 23.

¶ II. *Energetic Rebuke of the Galatians on Account of Their Abandonment of the Truth. i. 6–10.*

1. Expression of surprise at their fickleness=I marvel that you are so quickly removed from him who called you in the grace of Christ unto a different gospel; 6.

2. Explanation to avoid misconception=which is not another gospel; (A) only there are some that trouble you, (B) and would pervert the gospel of Christ. 7.

3. Fearful consequence of such perversion of the truth= But though we, or an angel from heaven, should preach unto you any gospel other than that which we preached unto you, let him be anathema. 8.

4. Emphatic repetition=(A) As we have said before, (A²) so say I now again, (B) if any man (a) preaches unto you any gospel other than that which you received, (b) let him be anathema. 9.

5. Personal ground of this intolerance=For (A) am I now persuading men? (B) or God? (A²) or am I seeking to please men? 10.

6. Justification of this refusal to conciliate men=If I were still pleasing men, I should not be a servant of Christ.

Queries.

(1). Why the extreme severity towards those who would pervert the gospel? 8, 9. *Cf.* Rom. i. 16.

(2). Reconcile ver. 10 with I. Cor. x. 33. Interpret in the light of the context of each.

¶ III. *Historic Evidence of his Independence of Men as to His Apostolic Commission and His Knowledge of the Gospel.* *i.' 11-24.*

1. Ground of his confidence in the truth of the gospel which he preached=For I make known to you, brethren, as touching the gospel which was preached by me, that it is not after man. 11.

2. Positive historic evidence of this=(A) For neither did I receive it from man, (A²) nor was I taught it, (B) but it came to me through revelation of Jesus Christ. 12.

3. This evinced from the historic fact that his previous hostility to the gospel precluded its communication from any one= For you have heard of my manner of life in time past in the Jews' religion, (A) how that beyond measure (a) I persecuted the church of God, (b) and made havock of it : (B) and I advanced in the Jews' religion beyond many of mine own age among my countrymen, (B²) being more exceedingly zealous for the traditions of my fathers. 13, 14.

4. Still further evinced by his subsequent lack of intercourse with religious teachers=But when it was the good pleasure of God, who set me apart, * even from my mother's womb, and called me through his grace, to reveal his Son in me, that I might preach him among the Gentiles ; (A) immediately, I conferred not with flesh and blood : (B) neither went I up to Jerusalem to those who were apostles before me : (a) but I went away into Arabia ; (b) and again I returned unto Damascus. 15-17.

5. This lack of opportunity expanded into a historic space of three years before seeing any apostle=Then after three years (A) I went up to Jerusalem (a) to visit Cephas, (b) and tarried with him fifteen days. (B) But other of the apostles (a) saw I none, (b) save James the Lord's brother. 18, 19.

---

* Green's rendering of the original verb.

6. Solemn avowal of truthfulness in giving this record=Now (A) touching the things which I write unto you, (B) behold, before God, I lie not. 20.

7. Continuation of the narrative showing subsequent lack of intercourse with all the original disciples=Then I came into the regions of Syria and Cilicia. (A) And I was still unknown by face unto the churches of Judæa which were in Christ : (B) but they only heard say, (a) He who once persecuted us (b) now preaches the faith of which he once made havock ; 21–23.

8. Their own consequent recognition of an independent divine work in his case=and they glorified God in me. 24.

Queries.

(1). How the apostle set apart to his work even from his birth? 15.

We have here another instance in which, by Metonymy, the virtual is represented as the actual, indicating in this case the divine purpose concerning Paul.

(2). How "conferred not with flesh and blood"? 16.

A Hebrew form of expression is used to signify that he learned nothing from man in his weakness, but from God alone. Compare as parallel Matt. xvi. 17.

(3). Who was "James, the Lord's brother"? 19. *Cf.* Matt. xiii. 55 ; Luke viii. 19, 20; John ii. 12. The "brethren" of Jesus mentioned in the first reference are shown by the other two to be constantly associated with Mary his mother as her actual sons.

(4). As according to John vii. 5 he was not one of the twelve, how can he here (ver. 19) and in Acts ix. 27 be called an apostle? *Cf.* Acts xiv. 14.

(5). Reconcile Paul's statement as to seeing only Peter and James, 19, with Luke's in Acts ix. 27 in giving an account of this visit to Jerusalem.

When Luke represents Barnabas as introducing Paul to "the apostles" on this occasion he evidently refers to all the apostles who were then in that city. "The notice," says Meyer, "that at that time Paul saw only Peter and James in Jerusalem does not conflict with the indefinite [expression] 'the apostles,' but authentically defines it."

¶ IV.   *The Recognition of his Independent Apostleship and Gospel of Freedom by the Other Apostles in Conference at Jerusalem. ii. 1–10.*

1. Occasion of his first important interview with the apostles=Then after the space of fourteen years I went up to Jerusalem (A) with Barnabas, (B) taking Titus also with me. 1.

2. This the result only of divine direction=And I went up by revelation ; 2.

3. His independent mode of procedure on his arrival=(A) and I laid before them the gospel which I preach among the Gentiles, (B) but privately before those who were of repute,

4. His motive in this as to ulterior effect in meeting opposition=lest by any means I should be running, or had run, in vain.

5. The wisdom of his procedure indicated through apostolic sanction of his teaching=But not even Titus who was with me, being a Greek, was compelled to be circumcised : 3.

6. Source of a legalistic effort at such compulsion=and that because of the false brethren privily brought in, (A) who came in privily to spy out our liberty which we have in Christ Jesus, (B) that they might bring us into bondage : 4.

7. Emphatic indication of his unyielding opposition to this =to whom we gave place in the way of subjection, no, not for an hour ; 5.

8. The important end in view=that the truth of the gospel might continue with you.

9. Indorsement of his course and recognition of his independent apostleship by the older apostles=(A) But [nothing was imparted to me] from those who were reputed to be somewhat ((a) whatsoever they were, it makes no matter to me : (b) God accepts not a man's person)—(A^2) they, I say, who were of repute imparted nothing to me : (B) but contrariwise, James and Cephas and John, they who were reputed to be pillars, gave to me and Barnabas the right hands of fellowship, (a) when they saw that I had been intrusted with the gospel of the uncircumcision, even as Peter with the gospel of the circumcision ((a^2) for he that wrought for Peter unto the apostleship of the circumcision wrought for me also unto the Gentiles) ; (b) when also they perceived the grace that was given unto me. 6–9.

10. Object in giving the hand in recognition of a gracious work among the Gentiles as divine as that among the Jews=(A) that we should go unto the Gentiles, (B) and they unto the circumcision ; 9.

11. The one obligation fraternally imposed, and heartily accepted by Paul, respecting the Jews=(A) only they would that we should remember the poor ; (B) which very thing I was also zealous to do. 10.

Queries.

(1). Why state that he went up to Jerusalem "by revelation" or divine direction? 2. Cf. 6, 8.

(2). Why think that he "should be running" in vain unless the older apostles would sanction his work? 2.

The right view is suggested in the analysis, yet a fuller explanation perhaps is demanded. Certainly he could not suppose that the wondrous success of his ministry depended on any human indorsement, for that success had already been accomplished. Nor could he seek to convince himself of the genuineness of his work by such approval, for this would amount to a confession of the dependence upon the other apostles alleged by his legalistic opponents and repudiated by him throughout this section of the Epistle. Moreover, if the manifest working of the divine hand in supernatural support of his ministry and in crowning it with abundant success accompanied even with clear declarations of approval from on high could not assure him of the righteousness and acceptability of his work, no expressed approbation by those "who were of repute" in the church could do so. Let us remember that Paul aimed at the establishment of the whole church in spiritual unity upon the broad basis of universal freedom in Christ and had the other apostles failed to perceive "the grace that was given" to him in apostolic power and efficiency his judaizing adversaries could have effectually used this in thwarting his efforts.

(3). Expose Baur's perversion of ver. 7 in representing the language as indicating a doctrinal difference between Paul and the other apostles.

| To interpret an expression in a way that neither the language employed nor the context will justify is unhermeneutical. || To force upon it an interpretation that is plainly contradicted by the passage itself and the context is utterly inexcusable. Now when

Paul represents himself as "intrusted with the gospel of the uncircumcision" as Peter had been "with the gospel of the circumcision"
he says afterwards that because of this he and Barnabas received
the hand of fellowship to "go unto the Gentiles" while Peter and
others were to minister mainly, "unto the circumcision." It is
only therefore a distinction as to their spheres of labor in preaching the same gospel, and not a distinction between two different
gospels, the one a gospel of Christian freedom offering blessings
to all without national or personal distinctions, and the other a
gospel of Jewish exclusiveness demanding submission to the law
of Moses as indispensable to salvation ! ! Peter was no preacher
of legal justification with which Paul's gospel of grace stood in
absolute contradiction. Two clear statements of Paul in this connection exclude such supposition and show the concord of these
apostles in their advocacy of one and the same gospel of the grace
of God. Notice, in the first place, that while Paul claimed to be
independent of the other apostles in receiving his apostolic commission and his knowledge of the truth, yet so far from placing
himself in opposition to them or pretending to preach another
gospel he ascribes his inspired teaching and that of Peter to *the
same divine source.* "He that *wrought for Peter* unto the apostleship of the circumcision *wrought for me also* unto the Gentiles." Is God the author of contradictions? Did he inspire
Peter to preach legalism and Paul to contradict him in preaching
salvation by grace? In the second place, notice the direct address
of Paul to Peter presented in ver. 15, 16. "We (you and I, Peter)
being Jews by nature, and not sinners of the Gentiles, yet *knowing that a man is not justified by the works of the law*, save
through faith in Jesus Christ, *even we* believed on Christ Jesus
*that we might be justified by faith in Christ and not by the works
of the law.*" Paul thus represents Peter and the other apostles
as fully ageed with him in repudiating justification by the works
of the law and in seeking for themselves, what they preached to
others, salvation through Christ alone. *

* Ferdinand Christian Baur was the founder of the Tubingen school of criticism. His effort to make out from the
second chapter of Galatians an irreconcilable difference between Paul and the other apostles, contrary to the record in
Acts of Apostles, which sets forth their doctrinal harmony, was meant to show that Acts is for the most part a fictitious
production not written by Luke but composed in the second century to cover up the doctrinal discords of the apostles
and heal up the consequent schism. Let this miserable specimen of "higher criticism," now exposed and antiquated
in a large measure in the land of its birth, be a warning to all who are ready to swallow the vagaries of critics of renown
because of their learning and their connection with some University. What is needed in our day, as perhaps in all
former days, is better exegesis and less reverence for the mere authority of scholarship.

¶ V. *Final Proof of His Apostolic Independence Incidentally Involving Anticipation of His Polemic against Legalism.*
ii. 11–21.

1. Reference to his opposition to Peter=But when Cephas came to Antioch, I resisted him to the face, 11.

2. Explanatory reason=because he stood condemned.

3. Ground of this charge=(A) For before that certain came from James, he did eat with the Gentiles : (B) but when they came, (a) he drew back (b) and separated himself, 12.

4. The cause of this assigned=fearing those who were of the circumcision.

5. Effect of this temporizing conduct=(A) And the rest of the Jews dissembled likewise with him ; (B) insomuch that even Barnabas was carried away with their dissimulation. 13.

6. Paul aroused by this to earnest remonstrance=(A) But when I saw that they walked not uprightly according to the truth of the gospel, (B) I said unto Cephas before them all, (a) if thou, being a Jew, livest as do the Gentiles, (a²) and not as do the Jews, (b) how compellest thou the Gentiles to live as do the Jews? 14.

7. Appeal to Peter's correct convictions for correction of his course=We being Jews by nature, and not sinners of the Gentiles, yet even we (A) believed on Christ Jesus, (a) that we might be justified by faith in Christ, (b) and not by the works of the law, (B) knowing (a) that a man is not justified by the works of the law, (b) save through faith in Jesus Christ : 15, 16.

8. Accepted axiom warranting their renunciation of legalism for Christ=because by the works of the law shall no flesh be justified.

9. Absurdity of attempting a combination of legalism with faith in Christ=(A) But if, (a) while we sought to be justified in Christ, (b) we ourselves also were found sinners, (B) is Christ a minister of sin? (B²) God forbid. 17.

10. Proof of the connection between such effort and the resulting sinful condition=(A) For if I build up again those things which I destroyed, (B) I prove myself a transgressor. 18.

11. Result by contrast of a complete renunciation as seen in Paul's own case=For I through the law (A) died unto the law, (B) that I might live unto God. 19.

12. Explanatory expansion of this=(A) I have been crucified with Christ; (B) yet (a) I live; (b) and yet no longer I, (b²)
but Christ lives in me: 20.

13. The anti-legalistic principle of this vital union=(A) and
that life which I now live in the flesh I live in faith, (B) the faith
which is in the Son of God, (a) who loved me, (b) and gave
himself up for me.

14. Its gracious character as exemplified in Paul=I do not
make void the grace of God: 21.

15. Ground for regarding such nullification of grace as
inherent in legalism=for if righteousness is through the law, then
Christ died for nought.

Queries.

(1). What expressions show that Peter's fault was one of
conduct not of conviction? *Cf.* ver. 12, 13, 14.

Had religious writers always considered that God is able to
make men *infallible as teachers* through inspiration without making them *perfect as men* through sanctification,* Christian literature would have been far less burdened than it is with crudities
touching this celebrated conflict of Paul with Peter. Witness
the controversy between Jerome and Augustine on this subject
embodied in the collected "Letters" of the latter. Jerome, following Origen in the matter, represented Paul as only *seeming*
to rebuke Peter through mutual understanding for only an *apparent* deviation from right with a view to conciliation. He asks:
"How could Paul have the assurance and effrontery to rebuke in
another what he had done himself?;" alluding to Paul's own
observance of Jewish customs to facilitate the progress of the
gospel among the Jews. Augustine with his sturdier common
sense and finer exegetical insight recognized the difference
between the free observance of customs in the interests of others
and the observance of them on the demand of legalists as a condition of salvation. And he clearly demonstrated that Jerome's
interpretation of the passage in hand would involve Paul in the
guilt of falsehood when he positively says of Peter and others
that on this occasion "they walked not uprightly according to
the truth of the gospel." This, he correctly argues, would dis-
credit the truth and authority of the word of God. "Better far,"

* Even a Balaam while attempting to curse Israel could be constrained by the prophetic Spirit to speak unerringly concerning the welfare of God's people.

he says, "that I should read with certainty and persuasion of its truth the Holy Scripture, and should, without questioning the trustworthiness of its statements, learn from it that men have been either commended or corrected or condemned, than that I should admit suspicions affecting the trustworthiness of the whole oracles of God." But a still more striking instance of a false exegesis of this passage appears in the apology which a Roman bishop, Pelagius II, in the sixth century makes for a doctrinal error of one of his predecessors in the papal chair. In a letter to the Istrian bishops as quoted by Bowen* he wrote as follows: "St. Peter, a greater apostle than St. Paul, long maintained the necessity of circumcision, subjecting the converted Gentiles to that Jewish and antiquated ceremony. But being convinced by St. Paul that he walked not uprightly according to the truth of the gospel, he changed his opinion. * * -. If the prime apostle held one doctrine while he was seeking after truth, and another after he had found it; if he changed his opinion as soon as he was made sensible of his error; why should a change of opinion be condemned in this See, while the like change is, by the whole church, commended and applauded in its founder?" Now here is a distinct acknowledgment by one who is now called a pope that occupants of the papal chair may in their teaching advocate erroneous doctrine, thus conceding papal fallibility contrary to the modern creed of the Roman Church. And Plagius himself proves his own fallibility by the very erroneous interpretation given by him of the passage before us. Popes may be "made sensible of error" in "doctrine" and so undergo "a change of opinion," but the inspired Peter being from first to last in full doctrinal agreement with the equally inspired Paul, as already seen from ver. 8 and 16, underwent no such change. How strange that many modern expositors of eminence fall into this error without, indeed, pushing it as far as Pelagius. Even so enlightened a scholar, so able an exegete, and safe a theologian as Ellicott speaks of the "retrogressive principles" of Peter.† Paul found no fault with the "principles" of Peter but with a line of conduct that *in effect* confirmed the demands of the legalists and put in jeopardy the religious privileges of the Gentiles.

---

* History of the Popes. Vol. I. p. 387. Edition of Cox.

† Commentary in loco.

(2). What meant by the expression that "certain came from James" and precipitated this issue at Antioch?

(a). It is not to be supposed that James authorized them to go to Antioch with a view of influencing Jewish believers to withdraw and separate themselves from their Gentile brethren who had not been circumcised. For James had already put himself on record in opposition to legalistic demands upon Gentile believers, Acts xv. 13–20, and afterwards confirmed this position in the advice which he gave to Paul. Acts xxi. 25. (b). But the probability is that the "certain" men who went out from James were sent by him on some business connected with the affairs of the church, or even that they came without a special commission from James from the midst of the community over which as an inspired guide of the church he was presiding, and that on reaching Antioch they allowed their Jewish predilections to exercise there such a controlling influence as to seriously affect the liberty of the gospel and the rights of the Gentile Christians.

(3). We here for the first time meet with the great axiom that "by the works of the law shall no flesh be justified." What the import of "justification" and its correlative, "righteousness"? 16.

When Paul asks, in Rom. viii. 33, "Who shall lay anything to the charge of God's elect?" he strongly denies by interrogation that any one can bring a charge or accusation in the case. He then gives the reason by saying, "It is God who justifies." By this connection of thought it is evident that justification is God's recognition of one as free from all accusation though standing before that law which is "holy, just and good." To declare this divine recognition of freedom from legal charge, or to treat one as thus exempt is to justify that person and the resulting state of justification, the divinely acknowledged uprightness of attitude toward the divine law, is called "righteousness."* If any being, an angel for example, has met in all its fulness every demand of the divine law, he may be declared righteous on that ground. This is legal justification as the law itself would justify such an observer of its requirements. If any one stands "in Christ" before the divine law, no charge or accusation can be brought against him, since God sees nothing "in Christ" to condemn. This is the only way in which an imperfect being like man can be regarded as free

---

* This word has other applications, but we speak of it here as a correlative of justification.

from accusation, and this is gracious justification on the ground
of "the redemption that is in Christ Jesus."

(4). With what amplitude of meaning does Paul use the
term "law" in his argument on justification?

We would very naturally, and properly, suppose that in a
discussion with Jews the word law would refer to the Mosaic
system. And, indeed, Paul's legalistic opponents tersely expressed
their creed in the following terms : "It is needful to circumcise"
all uncircumcised believers "and to charge them to keep the law
of Moses." In combating these the apostle's mind would, of
course, be upon this law, yet his grand argument soars, as we
shall see, into a higher region and deals with the ethical system
of Moses as only *a form* of the imperishable law on which is based
the whole moral government of God. Let it be understood in
the first place, that Paul in his opposition to Jewish legalists
makes no formal distinctions as to the nature of legal enactments,
but refers to the Mosaic system as a whole. He argues upon the
principle that one is "a debtor to do the whole law" who strives
after legal justification. "For it is written, Cursed is every one
who continues not in all things that are written in the book
of the law, to do them." Now the observance of the law as a
whole involves, of course, not only the keeping of its ritualistic
requirements—a thing quite possible in itself—but also its high
moral demands upon the heart and the life which no man, because
of human imperfection, can adaquately meet. *And it is precisely in this moral realm* that Paul's argument finds those insuperable difficulties that stand in the way of legal justification.
It is, therefore, not ceremonialism but legalism on the ethical
plane that Paul so strenuously combats. A man might observe
every requirement of even a very burdensome ritual and on this,
as a condition divinely appointed, be justified through the grace
of God in all its fulness and richness ; but a complete fulfilment
of the law's moral demands is unattainable by man, and if such
moral perfection could be reached by him, the justification thence
resulting could not be in any measure whatever a justification
through grace, but would rest wholly on human merit and legalistic claims. So completely, indeed, is this great argument occu-
pied with the moral aspects of the law that the apostle speaks of
Gentiles as doing "by nature the things of the law" and as having
its work "written in their hearts." Apart therefore from its

mere transitory ceremonial, including such elements as the Seventh Day and Circumcision, "the law of Moses" was but a form of the eternal divine law which in essence remains for ever obligatory for all the intelligences of the universe.

(5). What, accordingly, are those "works of the law" by which "shall no flesh be justified"?

To suppose as many do that obedience to any commandment or law whatever belongs to what Paul calls "the works of the law," without reference to when, or how, or by whom, or under what system that law or precept was enacted betrays a confusion of ideas that renders a comprehension of Paul's reasoning utterly impossible. To confound submission to the gracious precepts of the gospel of Christ with a legalistic course of life under a mere dispensation of law which would make void the grace of God and render abortive the death of his Son (ver. 21) is to blend into union the darkness of human error and the light of divine truth. To regard the gracious appointment of Christian baptism, for example, as an element of a legal system and submission to this requirement of the gospel as a work "in righteousness, which we did ourselves," a manifestation of our own righteouness, is to confound a trustful surrender to Christ and reliance on him with a self-righteous repudiation of him in a delusive dependence on human merit. Law, as standing in contrast with grace before the mind of Paul, denotes a purely legal system with its various enactments and penalties, standing wholly apart from, and incompatible with, the system of grace which has its own precepts along with merciful provisions for the benefit of sinful men. "The works of the law" are works done in obedience to the requirements of a legal system which instead of justifying pronounces a curse, Gal. iii. 10, upon every one who fails at any point in rendering a complete and faultless fulfilment of all its demands. It therefore knows no "works" of obedience short of absolute moral perfection, and as all men are sinful, Rom. iii. 23, there are no "works of the law" possible to man and hence for him no possible legal justification, Rom. iii. 20 . But to conclude from this that justification cannot be conditioned by divine appointment on submission to any requirement of the gospel of the grace of God is to confound things that are irreconcilable opposites.

(6). Explain the connection between ver. ~~18, 19.~~ *17, 18*

If after abandoning legalism for Christ as the only ground of justification one should return to rebuild the legal temple to find hope of acceptance therein, the very act of so doing would be a declaration that the previous abandonment of the law was sinful. And from this it would follow that Christ in offering salvation apart from the law would be a promoter of sin.

(7). How was it that "through the law" the apostle "died unto the law"? 19.

The next verse shows that the death to which reference is made was involved in his *crucifixion with Christ*. He thus, through the law's demand, under which Christ's redemptive death took place, died to the law's power to condemn or pronounce its "curse" according to iii. 13. Alford well paraphrases the passage as follows : "In Christ, who fulfilled the law, I died to the law, i. e., satisfied the law's requirements and passed out of its pale." This deeper sense of the believer's death through participation in the death of Christ is explicitly set forth in Rom. vi. 3, 4.

(8). What faith in Christ is here described as that by which Paul lived "unto God"? 20.

The concluding clause of the verse shows that it was not simply faith in the sinless life of Christ but faith in his atoning death. It was Christ "who loved me, and *gave himself up for me*."

(9). Show from what we have seen respecting justification by "the works of the law," that from its very nature it would "make void the grace of God" and render needless the death of his Son. 21.

SECTION SECOND.

The All-sufficiency of the Gospel and the Utter Insufficiency of the Law for the Justification of Men.

iii. 1–iv. 31.

¶ I. *Fervid Remonstrance with the Galatians for Their Inconsiderate Abandonment of the Only Means of Salvation. iii. 1–10.*

1. Folly of their course indicated=O foolish Galatians, who did bewitch you, before whose eyes Jesus Christ was openly set forth crucified? 1.

2. Argument evincing this folly grounded on an appeal to their experience=This only would I learn from you, (A) Received you the Spirit by the works of the law, (B) or by the message* of faith? 2.

3. Second argumentative appeal showing the absurdity of their course=Are you so foolish? (A) having begun in the Spirit, (B) are you now perfected in the flesh? 3.

4. Third appeal to their experience=(A) Did you suffer so many things in vain? (B) if it be indeed in vain. 4.

5. First argument in expanded form=He therefore that supplies to you the Spirit, and works miracles among you, (A) does he it by the works of the law, (B) or by the message of faith? 5.

6. Confirmation of the implied correct answer to these questions by the case of Abraham=(A) Even as Abraham believed God, (B) and it was reckoned unto him for righteousness. 6.

7. Logical conclusion as to other believers=Know therefore that they who be of faith, the same are sons of Abraham. 7.

8. This reasoning harmonious with the explicit teaching of Scripture=And the Scripture, (A) foreseeing that God would justify the Gentiles by faith, (B) preached the gospel beforehand unto Abraham, (B²) saying, In thee shall all the nations be blessed. 8.

9. Conclusion from this=So then they that be of faith are blessed with the faithful Abraham. 9

10. Evidence that only such are blessed=(A) For as many as are of the works of the law are under a curse: (B) for it is

---

* Marginal rendering preferred.

written, Cursed is every one who continues not in all things that
are written in the book of the law, to do them. 10.

Queries.

(1). Why the expression, "before whose eyes Jesus Christ
was openly set forth crucified"? 1.

It was suggested by the word "bewitch." "Who could
have bewitched you by his gaze, when you had only to fix your
eyes on Christ to escape the fascination?" Ellicott.

(2). How the word Spirit employed in the expression :
"Received you the Spirit by the works of the law, or by the message of faith"? 2. *Cf.* 5.

While the Spirit itself was received as the source of spiritual
blessings, reference is made here, as ver. 5 would indicate, to the
latter, to which by Metonymy the term Spirit is applied. Paul
asks the Galatians to testify from their experience as to whether
or not their spiritual blessings came to them apart from "the message of faith," the gospel of the grace of God, which as preached
by him they had accepted.

(3). What the antithesis in the expression : "Having begun
in the Spirit, are you now perfected in the flesh"? 3.

There is no room in the context with the continued contrast
before Paul's mind between the law and the gospel for the antithesis between the Holy Spirit and the unholy disposition of carnal
men which many exegetes regard as the matter to which reference is made by the apostle. The Galatians were drifting into
Judaism and the simple meaning of Paul's question is, Having
entered upon the spirituality of the economy of the gospel, are
you to find perfection in the graceless legalism of an effete system with its "carnal ordinances, imposed until a time of reformation"? This is not the only passage in which Judaism is called
"the flesh" in contrast with Christianity (*cf,* Philippians iii.
4-9), nor the only passage in which the gospel is called "the
spirit" in contrast with the legal system of the Jews. (*Cf.* II.
Cor. iii. 6-11.)

(4). How "preached the gospel beforehand unto Abraham"? 8.

The passage leaves no doubt as to what this preaching
was : "Saying, In thee shall all the nations be blessed." This is
a vague promise of blessing for all men to be fulfilled in after
days without indicating the high spirituality of the blessing or

explaining the elementary provisions of the gospel for effecting the fulfilment. The redemptive death of Christ and his resurrection in behalf of humanity were embraced in the promise but not revealed as yet. The gospel bud was presented to Abraham : the full-blown flower was not yet seen. Rom. xvi. 25, 26.

(5). How long had Abraham been walking by faith as a trusting obedient, accepted servant of God *before* the time to which reference is here made by Paul when it was said of him in Canaan (Gen. xv. 5, 6) that "he believed in the Lord; and he counted it to him for righteousness"? *Cf.* Heb. xi. 8-10 with Gen. xii. 1-8.

It will be seen from these references that he had thus lived in trustful submission to the will of God for years, even from the time when he received the divine call to go into Canaan. "By faith Abraham, when he was called, *obeyed to go out* unto a place which he was to receive for an inheritance ; and he *went out, not knowing whither he went.*" What an illustration of trusting, justifying faith? Still further : "By faith he became a sojourner in the land of promise, as in a land not his own, dwelling in tents, with Isaac and Jacob, the heirs with him of the same promise : for he looked for the city which hath the foundations, whose builder and maker is God." And it was during this time of earlier acceptable service that Abraham, first at Shechem and afterwards near Bethel (Gen. xii. 7, 8), "builded an altar unto the Lord, and called upon the name of the Lord." Accordingly, as a result of such a life of trust and obedience to the divine will God gave to Abraham renewed assurance of acceptance just before the transaction mentioned by Paul. For "the word of the Lord came unto Abram in a vision, saying, Fear not, Abram : I am thy shield, and thy exceeding great reward." Gen. xv. 1. It was thus that Abraham walked obediently before God, and thus that he received the divine testimonial of continued acceptance.

(6.) Show how the hermeneutical "Law of Opposition" has often been set at nought by a false representation of Abraham's justification by faith without legalistic works. 11, 12.

Paul argues that Abraham was justified by faith apart from *the works of the law* which last would be, not a *mere condition*, but an *independent ground* of justification, involving meritorious claims upon God. From this the conclusion is sometimes most illogically

drawn that Abraham's justification by faith was without the appropriate *works of faith itself* which could only constitute *the gracious condition* divinely appointed on which unmerited salvation
would be bestowed as a gift. The false reasoning with its con-
fused exegesis loses sight of the real contrast of opposites before
Paul's mind, and constructs a fictitious contrast or opposition that
is utterly foreign to the thought of the apostle.

(7). Show from ver. 10 that legalistic morality in sinless
perfection is the *sole ground*, standing wholly apart from Christ
and from grace, on which a legal system will justify any being;
and that therefore it is preposterous to apply to any act of faith
or divinely appointed condition of favor what is anywhere affirmed
of "the works of the law." 10.

¶ II.   *Further Evidence of the Incompetency of the Law for the
Justification of Men. iii. 11–18.*

1.   Proposition to be established=Now that no man is justified by the law in the sight of God, is evident : 11.

2.   Scriptural premises from which this is deducible as a
conclusion=(A) for, "the righteous shall live by faith ;" (Hab.
ii. 4) (B) and the law is not of faith ; (B²) but, "He that does
them shall live in them." 11, 12. See Lev. xviii. 5.

3.   The *gracious ground* of the blessing here *graciously conditioned* on faith=(A) Christ redeemed us from the curse of the
law, (B) having become a curse for us : (B²) for it is written,
Cursed is every one who hangs on a tree : 13.

4.   Gracious ends subserved by this=(A) that upon the Gentiles might come the blessing of Abraham in Christ Jesus; (B)
that we might receive the promise of the Spirit through faith. 14.

5.   The nature of a covenant promise indicated=Brethren,
I speak after the manner of men : (A) Though it be but a man's
covenant, (B) yet when it has been confirmed, (a) no man makes
it void, (b) or adds thereto. 15.

6.   As divinely confirmed the terms of the covenant with
Abraham remain unalterable in the exclusion of Jewish claims=
(A) Now to Abraham were the promises spoken, and to his seed.
(B) He says not, (a) And to seeds, (a²) as of many ; (b) but as
of one, (b²) And to thy seed, which is Christ. 16.

7.   As thus unalterable these terms suffered no change on
the giving of the law=Now this I say ; A covenant confirmed

beforehand by God, the law, (A) which came four hundred and thirty years after, (B) does not disannul, (B²) so as to make the promise of none effect. 17.

8.　Proof found in this that the promised inheritance is not grounded on legal claims=For if the inheritance is of the law, (A) it is no more of promise : (B) but God has granted it to Abraham by promise. 18.

Queries.

(1).　State the difference between justification by law and justification by faith under the contrast presented in ver. 11, 12.

In the apostle's argument here for gracious, as opposed to legal, justification we have all the elements of a regular syllogism, whose premises are taken from the Old Testament. "The righteous shall live by faith." But "the law is not of faith." Therefore the righteous shall not live by the law ; or "no man is justified by the law in the sight of God." As he had quoted the major premise—"The righteous shall live by faith"—from Hab. ii. 4, he supports the minor premise—"The law is not of faith"—by a quotation from Lev. xviii. 5 which says in full : "You shall therefore keep my statutes and my judgments : which if a man do, he shall live in them." The contrast is between living through faith, on the one hand, and living in the doing of the law's requirements, on the other. A man might, in a relative sense or according to his ability, observe the law just as Moses intended ; but the law requires more than this if it is to be the ground and source of justification. Legal justification is not merely conditioned, but absolutely grounded, on a faultless and meritorious doing of all the demands of the law. There is therefore for man no possible justification of this kind. Righteousness for him, acceptance with his God, can only be *grounded on Christ* and *conditioned on a fruitful and operative faith in him*. The contrast between *doing* and *believing* in the passage before us is a contrast between *legal obedience* apart from faith, on the one hand, and *obedient faith* in the Lord Jesus, on the other. *Cf.* Rom. iv. 12. Paul was never so thoughtless as to draw a contrast between faith itself and any of its active manifestations. These all belong to the system of grace as opposed to a Christless, graceless, faithless system of legal works.

(2). Explain the nature of the redemptive or atoning work of Christ as set forth in 13.

(3). Vindicate against the charge of rationalists Paul's interpretation of the promise to Abraham. 16.

The Apostle argues that, in the employment of the word "seed" in the singular in the giving of the promises, or the repeated promise, the reference is to Christ and not to the Jewish people in general. "He says not, And to seeds, as of many; but as of one, And to thy seed, which is Christ." It is not astonishing that Baur who, as we have seen, professed to find a doctrinal disagreement between Paul and Peter where the very reverse is set forth, should here represent the reasoning of Paul as "plainly arbitrary and incorrect," and he voices the decision of many rationalistic expositors. Even Meyer represents the apostle as falling into a mere "Rabbinical method" of interpretation. Jerome of the ancients represents him as using a "foolish" argument as one who is reasoning with the "foolish Galatians"–a strange way indeed to cure them of their folly! In contrast with these disparaging utterances is the truthful and just representation of Ellicott: "Nevertheless, we have here an interpretation which the apostle, writing under the illumination of the Holy Spirit has deliberately propounded, and which, therefore (whatever difficulties may at first appear in it), is profoundly and indisputably true." Yet neither Ellicott, nor any other commentator known to me, has brought out clearly the true meaning of the apostle in refutation of the rationalistic charge against his teaching in this passage. The objectors allege, and very correctly, that the term "seed" is a collective noun and may consequently denote a multitude of persons without taking the plural form. They thence infer that Paul here ignores usage and falls into fallacious reasoning, supposing that he means to exclude the Jews as *many persons* descended from Abraham and to argue from the singular form of the term "seed" in the promise that, accordingly, reference is made to only *one person*, one descendant of Abraham, Christ. If such indeed is really the apostle's meaning the point is well taken against his contention. But it is precisely in this false interpretation of Paul's argument that the imaginary difficulty exclusively lies. He does not interpret the language of the promise as pointing to Christ as one descendant of Abraham in contrast with many descendants from him, or many persons of whom his posterity is composed. For in ver. 29 while still commenting on the terms of this promise he represents the word "seed," using it in the singular, as denoting *a plurality of persons*. "If you be Christ's, then are you Abraham's seed, heirs according to the promise." Now how could Paul represent this word as excluding in the promise a plurality of persons, and immediately afterwards represent it as used in the same promise to denote such plurality? This shows the rationalistic interpretation of Paul's reasoning to be false and consequently demolishes the false charge grounded thereon. What then is the real contrast of unity and plurality before the mind of the apostle? Before he is through with his subject he makes the matter clear enough. In the next chapter he tell us that Abraham had two sons which allegorically represented two very distinct kinds of posterity. Ishmael represented Abraham's seed according to the flesh, the Jewish people as descended from him. Isaac represented Abraham's spiritual seed as summed up in Christ. In view of this he asks : "what says the Scripture? Cast out the handmaid and her son ; for the son of the handmaid *shall not inherit with the son of the freewoman*." Here then are two seeds, two kinds of posterity and the seed according to the flesh, as such, can have no part with the spiritual seed in the inheritance promised. Paul argues that if the Jews could claim the inheritance on the principle of fleshly connection with Abraham as his seed the terms of the promise should indicate it by the use of the plural "seeds" to include both kinds of posterity instead of the one kind embraced in spiritual unity in Christ—the one kind which Christ represents and includes as one in him where "there can be neither Jew nor Greek, there can be neither bond nor free," * * * "for ye all are one man in Christ Jesus." ver. 28. The word seed when used in the plural denotes plurality of kinds, not of individuals which may be signified by the word in the singular, as when we speak of a sower of seed, but a dealer in seeds. A good illustration of this distinction in the use of this term is found in Matt. xiii. 31, 32, "The kingdom of heaven is like unto a grain of mustard seed, which a man took, and sowed in his field : which indeed is less than all seeds," i. e., smaller than all other *kinds* of seed.*

---

* When the author, years ago, first led a class in exegesis through the Epistle to the Galatians he gave the exposition of ver. 16 presented above and has found no reason since then to modify his conclusions.

(4).   How the inheritance not of the law as being an inheritance by promise? 18.

Whatever comes through promise is received as a gift and is thus by grace.   That which is based on legal claims is of a different nature, as involving a personal right.

¶ III.   *The Design and Significance of the Law.   iii. 19–29.*

1.   Inquiry as to the import of the law═What then is the law? 19.

2.   Answer indicating its relation to sin, on the one hand, and to grace, on the other═It was added (A) because of transgressions, (B) till the seed should come to whom the promise has been made;

3.   Manner of its establishment═and it was ordained (A) through angels, (B) by the hand of a mediator.

4.   Argument based on this fact evincing the superiority of the promise as without mediation═Now a mediator (A) is not a mediator of one, (B) but God is one. 20.

5.   False inference obviated═(A) Is the law then against the promises of God? (B) God forbid: 21.

6.   Justification of this negative answer═(A) for if there had been a law given which could make alive, (B) verily righteousness would have been of the law.

7.   The real purpose of the law as preparatory set forth═Howbeit (A) the Scripture has shut up all things under sin, (B) that the promise by faith in Jesus Christ might be given to those who believe. 22.

8.   Consequent description of the state of men under the law before the revelation of grace═But before the faith * came, (A) we were kept in ward under the law, (B) shut up unto the faith which should afterwards be revealed. 23.

9.   Conclusion as to the office of the law═So that the law has been our tutor to bring us unto Christ, 24.

10.   The great end thus to be gained═that we might be justified by faith.

11.   Consequent description of the believer's condition under grace═But now that faith has come, (A) we are no longer under a tutor. (B) For you are all sons of God, through faith, in Christ Jesus. 25, 26.

---

* Marginal rendering preferred.

12. Explanatory reason=For (A) as many of you as were baptized into Christ (B) did put on Christ. 27.

13. Consequent oneness of all who are in him=(A) There can be neither Jew nor Greek, (B) there can be neither bond nor free, (C) there can be no male and female: (A B C) for you all are one man in Christ Jesus. 28.

14. Conclusion from this=(A) And if you are Christ's (B) then you are Abraham's seed, (B²) heirs according to promise. 29.

Queries.

(1). Import of the statement that the law was "added because of transgressions"? 19. *Cf.* Rom. iii. 20; vii. 7, 13.

From these references we learn that the law can lead men to the discovery of sin, but cannot remove it and so bring peace. But by thus revealing the real condition of the sinner it may lead him to look to Christ as the only source of spiritual life.

(2). In stating the difference between the promise and the law, how say in the case of the former that "God is one"? 20.

The law was given through Moses as a mediating agent. The promise was given to Abraham directly or without any mediation. Mediation implies two parties besides the mediator himself as a third person in the case. But in the case of the promise God was one party and the only one on the side of giving. He thus came into nearness to Abraham as the recipient of the promise. In the giving of the law, on the other hand, he stood at a remote position transmitting it first through angels and next to these through Moses on down to his people Israel.

(3). How has the Scripture "shut up all things under sin"? 22.

As may be seen from quotations made in Rom. iii. 10-18 the Scriptures demonstrate the hopelessness of man's condition under a mere legal system in manifesting the impossibility of his escape from the law's condemnation apart from the gracious provisions in Christ, or "until the seed should come to whom the promise was made." They thus show all in that condition to be "kept in ward under the law, shut up unto the faith which should afterwards be revealed." The ancient servants of God were indeed provisionally accepted but were never perfected for the final inheritance till the economy of grace was established. See Heb. ix. 15; xi. 39, 40.

(4). What do we learn from ver. 27 as to the relation of baptism to justification by faith and becoming sons of God in Christ? See also Rom. vi. 3, 4 as compared with Rom. iii. 24.

In commenting on this verse the great reforming advocate of justification by faith as opposed to meritorious works, Martin Luther, shows how far baptism in his estimation stood aloof from such works and how clearly he saw from this passage the connection of the ordinance with justification. He says: "To put on Christ according to the gospel means, not to put on the law and its righteousness, but means, by baptism, to receive the unspeakable treasure, namely, forgiveness of sins, righteousness, peace, comfort, joy in the Holy Spirit, blessedness, life and Christ himself with all that he is and has."

¶ IV. *The Difference between Man's Minority under Legal and Other Preparatory Discipline, on the One Hand, and the Fulness of His Privileges under Grace, on the Other. iv. 1–11.*

1. Minority described=But I say (A) that so long as the heir is a child, (a) he differs nothing from a bondservant, (b) though he be lord of all; (B) but (a) is under guardians and stewards (b) until the term appointed of the father. 1, 2.

2. Spiritual application=So we also, (A) when we were children,* (B) were held in bondage under the rudiments of the world: 3.

3. Consequent divine interposition in man's behalf=(A) but when the fulness of the time came, (B) God sent forth his Son, (a) born of a woman, (b) born under the law, 4.

4. The great end in view=(A) that he might redeem those who were under the law, (B) that we might receive the adoption of sons. 5.

5. The blessing consequent on the bestowal of sonship= And because you are sons, God sent forth the Spirit of his Son into our hearts, crying, Abba, Father. 6.

6. Logical conclusion from the whole argument=(A) So that (a) thou art no longer a bondservant, (b) but a son; (B) and if a son, then an heir through God. 7.

7. Contrast between their former state and their present position to indicate the folly of their backward inclination=(A) Howbeit at that time, (a) not knowing God, (b) you were in

---

* i. e., minors.

bondage to those which by nature are no gods : (B) but now (a) that you have come to know God, (a²) or rather to be known of God, (b) how turn you back again to the weak and beggarly rudiments, whereunto you desire to be in bondage over again? 8, 9.

8. Evidence of the declension here reproved=You observe days, and months, and seasons, and years. 10.

9. Consequent unfavorable impression on the apostle's mind =(A) I am afraid of you, (B) lest by any means I have bestowed labor upon you in vain. 11.

Queries.

(1). What figure used in representing a minor as "lord of all" of a prospective inheritance? 1.

(2). What the nature of the "bondage under the rudiments of the world"? 3. *Cf.* iii. 22–24.

There may, indeed, be a sort of needless bondage to a burdensome ritualism in a punctilious observance of forms and ceremonial requirements of an antiquated system, and many seem to think that this is the religious thralldom which Paul so earnestly opposes in this Epistle and some other writings. But although the Galatians were already observing Jewish seasons and sabbaths (10) the apostle does not regard them as involved as yet in the bondage toward which they were rapidly drifting. It is "the desire to be in bondage over again" (ver. 9) that he now condemns. "The Galatians," says Ellicott, "had been slaves to the rudiments in the form heathenism ; now they were desiring to enslave themselves *again* to the rudiments and to *commence* them *anew* in the form of Judaism." Now Paul had already described this legal form of bondage in iii. 22–24 as a state in which men were "kept in ward under the law" and "shut up" under sin while awaiting the redemption of the economy of grace. They were thus "in bondage" under "the curse of the law" from which Christ has now happily redeemed all who acknowledge his claims and accept the rich benefits of his grace.

(3). In referring to this great redemptive work of Christ why speak of him as "born of a woman" and "born under the law"? 4.

To represent God he must needs be divine and to represent man he must needs become human. Heb. ii. 14–18.   And to remove for man "the curse of the law" (iii. 13) he must of necessity come to man's position under the law, and thus redeem him from the law's condemnation. *Cf.* II. Cor. v. 21.

(4). Distinguish the sending of the Spirit into the heart of God's "sons" (ver. 6) from the converting agency of the Spirit in bringing men to sonship, and each of these also from what is called a baptism in the Holy Spirit.

On Pentecost we find all three standing apart from one another in point of time and differing as to their respective subjects, having a marked difference of purpose, and characterized by a difference of manifestation. In the first place there was the baptism in the Spirit of which the apostles were the subjects with the view, as previously announced by the Saviour, of their supernatural qualification for their grand work. Then came the converting influence of the Spirit through their inspired words confirmed by supernatural attestation addressed to the eye by which three thousand were convicted of sin and made believers in the Messiahship of Jesus as explained by Peter. Finally these were told to obey the gospel to obtain remission attended with the promise that they should then "receive the gift of the Holy Spirit." This corresponds exactly with the teaching of Paul in the passage before us : "Because you are sons [not to make you such], God sent forth the Spirit of his Son into your hearts."   And of this gift of the Spirit Jesus says (Jno. xiv. 17) that "the world cannot receive" it.

¶ V.   *Affectionate Appeal for an Earnest Hearing Based on*
        Past Association and Fellowship. iv. 12–20.

1. Dissuasion from Judaism through the force of his own example=I beseech you, brethren, (A) be as I am, (B) for I am as you are. 12.

2. Enforcement of the intreaty by reference to their past deportment=You did me no wrong :

3. Proof of their former kindness=but you know that because of an infirmity of the flesh I preached the gospel unto you the first time : (A) and that which was a temptation to you in my flesh (a) you despised not, (b) nor rejected; (B) but you received me (a) as an angel of God, (b) even as Christ Jesus. 13, 14.

4.   Transitory character of this good disposition=Where then is that gratulation of yourselves? 15.

5.   Evidence of this felicitation=for I bear you witness, that, if possible, you would have plucked out your eyes and given them to me. 15.

6.   The change in their regard for him inexcusable=(A) So then am I become your enemy, (B) because I tell you the truth? 16.

7.   The uncandid course of their Judaizing leaders described in contrast with his own candid way of dealing with them=(A) They zealously seek you in no good way; (B) nay, (a) they desire to shut you out, (b) that you may seek them. 17.

8.   The proper method of dealing described=But it is good to be zealously sought (A) in a good matter (B) at all times, (B²) and not only when I am present with you. 18.

9.   Their course due to their undeveloped state=My little children, (A) of whom I am again in travail (B) until Christ be formed in you, 19.

10.   Consequent expression of a wish concerning them=(A) yea, I could wish to be present with you now, (B) and to change my voice; 20.

11.   Source of this wish=for I am perplexed about you.

Queries.

(1).   Import of the expression : "be as I am, for I am as you are"? 12.

(2).   What exclusion by the Judaizers to which reference is made in ver. 17?   Context.

(3).   What the nature and force of the figure in ver. 19?

(4).   How speak of Christ as "formed in" them? 19.

Consider this in the light of their special needs and compare ii. 21 and iii. 1-3.

¶ VI.   *The Law and the Gospel in Allegory.   iv. 21-31.*

1.   Intimation that the law itself condemns the course of the legalists=Tell me, you that desire to be under the law, do you not hear the law? 21.

2.   Confirmatory reference to its teaching through Abraham's family=For it is written, that Abraham had two sons, (A) one by the handmaid, (B) and one by the freewoman. 22.

3.   Instructive difference between the births of the two sons =Howbeit (A) the son by the handmaid is born after the flesh; (B) but the son by the freewoman is born through promise. 23.

4.   Spiritual significance of these mothers and their sons= Which things contain an allegory : 24.

5.   Explanation=for these women are two covenants;

6.   Description of the first under this point of view=one from mount Sinai, (A) bearing children unto bondage, (B) which is Hagar.

7.   Resulting contrast between the two=(A) Now this Hagar is mount Sinai in Arabia, (a) and answers to the Jerusalem that now is : (b) for she (i. e. Jerusalem) is in bondage with her children.   (B) But the Jerusalem that is above, (a) is free, (b) which is our mother. 25, 26.

8.   Scriptural confirmation=For it is written, (A) Rejoice, thou barren that bearest not ; (A²) Break forth and cry, thou that travailest not : (B) for more are the children of the desolate than of her which has the husband. 27.

9.   Isaac analagous in birth to Christians=Now we, brethren, as Isaac was, are children of promise. 28.

10.   Ishmael analagous in birth and in spirit to legalistic Jews=(A) But as then he that was born after the flesh persecuted him that was born after the Spirit, (B) even so it is now. 29.

11.   Consequent rejection of the latter and admission of the former to the inheritance=Howbeit what says the Scripture? (A) Cast out the handmaid and her son : (B) for the son of the handmaid shall not inherit with the son of the freewoman. 30.

12.   Conclusion=Wherefore, brethren, (A) we are not children of a handmaid, (B) but of the freewoman. 31.

Queries.

(1).   Present the twelve analogies and twelve antitheses of this allegory. 21–31.

(A). **Mothers.**	The Handmaid=The Old Covenant. 24.	
	versus	*versus*
	The Freewoman=The New Covenant. 26, 31.	
(B). **Sons.**	Ishmael = Jews under the Old.	
	versus	*versus*
	Isaac = Christians under the New.	
(C). **Births.**	By Nature = Natural Birth. as to of the Ishmael Subjects of the Old. 29.	
	vs.	*vs.*
	Through Promise = Spiritual Birth. as to of the Isaac Subjects of the New. 28.	
(D). **Dispositions.**	Ishmael a Persecutor=Jewish Persecution. 29.	
	versus	*versus*
	Isaac's Endurance = Christian Endurance.	
(E). **States.**	Domestic Bondage = Legal Bondage. 25. as to of Ishmael The Jews.	
	vs.	*vs.*
	Domestic Freedom = Spiritual Liberty. 31. as to of Isaac Christians.	
(F). **Results.**	Ishmael "Cast Out"=Rejection of Jews. 30.	
	versus	*versus*
	Isaac Made Heir=Acceptance of Christians. 30.	

(2). On what ground must we regard the relationships in Abraham's family and the connected events as having an allegorical significance?

We need no other ground, and can have none higher, than the inspiration of Paul. To represent his interpretation of these things as simply "Rabbinical" or "merely subjective" and fanciful is to reduce this great authoritative "ambassador" of Christ to the level of ordinary writers and teachers. The allegorical follies and whimsical expositions of Origen and his followers in the early church by which they converted most of Old Testament history into riddles find no parallel whatever in an inspired apostle's acceptance of Scriptural narratives as really historical and his authoritative assertion under divine illumination that this or that event possesses a typical or an allegorical significance. "How various persons take this allegorical comment of the apostle," says Alford, "depends very much on their views of his authority as a Scripture interpreter. To those who receive the law as a great system of prophetic figures, there can be no difficulty in believing the events by which the giving of the law was prepared to have been prophetic figures also : not losing thereby any of their historic reality, but bearing to those who were able to see it aright this deeper meaning. * * * That the Rabbis and the Fathers, holding such deeper senses, should have often missed them, and allegorized fancifully and absurdly, is nothing to the purpose : it is surely most illogical to argue that because they were wrong, St. Paul cannot be right. The only thing which really does create any difficulty in my mind, is, that commentators with spiritual discernment, and appreciation of such a man as our apostle, should content themselves with quietly casting aside his Scripture interpretation wherever, as here, it passes their comprehension." In conclusion we may settle upon this as hermeneutically safe, that where inspiration has not spoken, yet where sufficient analogy seems to justify it, an uninspired man may regard it as *probable* that a Scripture event is allegorical as well as historical; but he cannot consider his conclusion in the case as having any doctrinal value or found thereon any exegetical argument.

(3). In the light of this allegory, what lesson is deducible from the difference between the births of the two sons and from

the consequent casting out of Hagar and Ishmael from all pros-
pect of inheritance?

Those who suppose that the Church of the New Testament
had its organic beginning in the family of Abraham and simply
realized its completeness after the coming of Christ would do
well to study the lessons of this allegory.   That the gospel in the
form of unexplained and unfulfilled promise of spiritual blessing
through his seed was announced to Abraham has already been
seen from iii. 8 and its context.   It is there made clear that this
promise of undefined spiritual blessing only vaguely embodied
"the faith which should afterwards be revealed."   Now the supposition that on the basis of this unexplained promise, whose spiritual contents remained to be "afterwards revealed" in and
through Christ, a "spiritual society" was organized in the family
of Abraham constituting what Calvin calls a *"vera ecclesia,"* is
not only a fiction of modern theology but is palpably at variance
with Paul's teaching in the allegory before us.   Let it be carefully noted that while Isaac, as the child of promise and born
unto freedom, allegorically represented the future spiritual seed
of Abraham as children by faith and heirs through Christ of the
spiritual inheritance (iii. 29), it was nevertheless through Isaac
himself that the kind of posterity came which Ishmael allegorically represented—*the offspring of Abraham according to the flesh,*
and hence debarred, as such, from all inheritance *in the spiritual
sense* of the promise.   Isaac as the son of Sarah became heir of
the temporal inheritance from which Ishmael as the son of
Hagar the bondwoman was actually excluded and this exclusion,
according to Paul's understanding, represented the exclusion of
Isaac's descendants, or Abraham's natural posterity through Isaac,
from all participation, as mere descendants of his, from the spiritual inheritance to be obtained through Christ.   Thus all of
Isaac's descendants, the whole Jewish people as subsequently
organized under the legal covenant at Sinai, were subjects of
that covenant which bore "children unto bondage" and so were
"kept in ward under the law, shut up unto the faith which was
afterwards to be revealed" on the coming of Christ.   Who now
were left in Abraham's family to be organized into a "Gospel
Church" on the basis of an undefined promise of something not
even revealed under that dispensation?   All Jews stood in covenant relation with the God of Abraham simply because they were

"born after the flesh," as the patriarch's offspring by nature, and all those carnal institutions, like circumcision, which were connected with his history belong, by their very nature, not to the spiritual side of the promise, which found fulfilment only in the Messianic kingdom, but to the carnal side alone, and were ultimately embraced in the national covenant at Mt. Sinai. Hence Jesus speaks of circumcision as an element of the law of Moses. Jno. vii. 23. Now, "What says the Scripture? Cast out the handmaid and her son: for the son of the handmaid shall not inherit with the son of the freewoman." As interpreted by Paul: abrogate the old covenant with its carnal provisions, and set aside its subjects, who, as "born after the flesh," shall not inherit with the spiritual children of the new covenant, who are heirs through Christ on the principle of faith. Those, therefore, who now claim to be "really and truly born citizens of the visible commonwealth of Christ, as they are born citizens of the commonwealth of the United States or of Great Britain,"* virtually abandon Christianity for Judaism, or blindly blend together the two incompatible administrations. By the clear provisions of the new covenant itself, which was typified by Sarah, and predicted as still in the future by Jeremiah, though indefinitely embodied in the promise to Abraham on its spiritual side, the principle of flesh with its consequence of infant membership, is distinctly repudiated, as having no place in the church of the New Testament. "Behold, the days come, says the Lord, That I will make a new covenant with the house of Israel and with the house of Judah: Not according to the covenant that I made with their fathers in the day that I took them by the hand to lead them forth out of the land of Egypt. * * — For this is the covenant that I will make with the house of Israel after those days, says the Lord; I will put my laws into their mind, and on their heart also will I write them: And I will be to them a God, And they shall be to me a people: And they shall not teach every man his fellow-citizen And every man his brother, saying, Know the Lord; For all shall know me, From the least to the greatest of them." Heb. viii. 8–12; Jer. xxxi. 31–34. Now, even supposing "the Gospel Church," or Messiah's kingdom, to have had its beginning under the Old Testament, we have here a new constitution, with new provisions of citizenship, in

---

* Discourses of Redemption, by Stuart Robinson. P. 86.

accordance with which, none shall be citizens, who are *too little* to "*know the Lord*," as having come in by natural birth; but must enter as having the laws of God "put into their mind," and written upon their heart, and are thus able to know the Lord "from the least to the greatest of them." We add that innocent babes can, through the Redeemer's reversal of the Adamic overthrow, enter the kingdom above, without the instrumentality of a covenant or a church. Rom. v. 15-19.

SECTION THIRD.

HORTATORY ENFORCEMENT OF DUTIES CONNECTED WITH THE POSSESSION OF CHRISTIAN FREEDOM.

v. 1-vi. 18.

¶ I. *Enslavement to the Law through Circumcision Involves a Practical Abandonment of Christ and the Gospel. v. 1-12.*

1. The maintenance of their liberty in Christ enjoined= With freedom did Christ set us free : (A) Stand fast therefore, (B) and be not entangled again in a yoke of bondage.* 1.

2. Argument evincing the folly of the opposite course= Behold, I Paul say unto you, that, (A) if ye receive circumcision, (B) Christ will profit you nothing. 2.

3. Additional argument from the obligation assumed in circumcision=Yea, I testify to every man that receives circumcision, that he is a debtor to do the whole law. 3.

4. Explanation of the truth just affirmed=(A) Ye are severed from Christ, ye who would be justified by the law. (B) ye are fallen away from grace. 4.

5. Ground on which this lapse from Christ is prevented= For we through the Spirit by faith wait for the hope of righteousness. 5.

6. Explanatory reason=For in Christ Jesus (A) neither circumcision avails anything, (A²) nor uncircumcision ; (B) but faith working through love. 6.

7. Consequent censure of their course as inexcusable=(A) Ye were running well ; (B) who did hinder you that you should not obey the truth? 7.

---

* I do not regard this first verse of the fifth chapter as the conclusion of the foregoing section of the Epistle but the proper beginning of the last or hortatory section. though by very many it is attached to the preceding or second section. Paul had shown that liberty results from union with Christ and he now begins the practical part of the Epistle by exhorting the Galatians to maintain the freedom thus obtained.

8. Their spiritual declension accounted for=(ᴀ) This persuasion came not of him that calls you. (ʙ) A little leaven leavens the whole lump. 8, 9.

9. Consequent censure of their leaders rather than the Galatians themselves=I have confidence to you-ward in the Lord, (ᴀ) that ye will be none otherwise minded; (ʙ) but he that troubles you shall bear his judgment, whosoever he be. 10.

10. Disclaims for himself any responsibility in the case= But I, brethren, if I still preach circumcision, (ᴀ) why am I still persecuted? (ʙ) then has the stumblingblock of the cross been done away. 11.

11. Expression of a wish as regards the seducers=I would that they who unsettle you would even cut themselves off. 12.

Queries.

(1). What the "freedom" received in and through Christ referred to here? ver. 1. *Cf.* iii. 13.

This freedom is the opposite of the "yoke of bondage," i. e., the yoke of the law, with which it here stands in contrast. The *nature* of this bondage has been explained in what was said on iv. 9. It is not enough to say that we are liberated through Christ from the claims of the law, unless it be understood that those claims, as of a legal system apart from grace, include the demand of moral perfection of which man is incapable, and hence involve the law's condemnation or curse in consequence of man's failure to meet perfectly its requirements. Freedom, therefore, from the whole legal system is implied in the expression "Christ redeemed us from the curse of the law." From the apostle's immediate reference to circumcision, in the passage before us, many hastily conclude that the freedom of which he speaks is exemption from the hardship of submission to this rite, and in general from the burden of ritualistic requirements. It is clear, however, from verse 3 that Paul speaks not of circumcision as an isolated act, but considered as a pledge to do the whole law in order to justification: and hence, to an impracticable demand, which, not being fulfilled, entails cursing instead of blessing. In one point of view, indeed, the enforcement of circumcision itself, as of any other religiously obsolete practice, is an intolerable wrong and a sin both against the church of Christ and against him as its sole Head and sovereign Ruler. As the rite ceased to be religiously binding with the abrogation of the Mosaic system, to enforce it any longer as obligatory or make it conditional to salvation is to do so simply on the ground of man's authority and thus elevate the human to the position of the divine in religion. This is Rome's great crime against Christ and his people in burdening the conscience with a multitude of requirements proceeding solely from her own will and usurpation of authority while pretending to give law in the name of the Lord Jesus.

(2). Reconcile with the statements concerning circumcision in ver. 2, 3, Paul's own act in circumcising Timothy. Acts xvi. 1–3.

Consider in the light of Acts xv. 1, 5, the respect in which Paul, in his opposition to legalists, condemns here the practice of circumcision and apply the Law of Opposition; then notice the vastly different point of view under which Timothy was circumcised. Acts xvi. 3.

(3). How "wait for the hope of righteousness"? 5.

Hope stands, by Metonymy, for its objective realization, in the final consummation of righteousness. *Cf.* Rom. viii. 24, 25.

(4). What, according to verse 6, is the faith that "avails," and consequently, which Paul, has all along, been contrasting with legalistic works?

As it is a "faith *working* through love," it is not an abstract faith, however genuine, which is often absurdly placed in contrast with its own practical manifestations. It was not simply the faith, hope and love of the Thessalonians, that Paul commended, but their "*work* of faith and *labour* of love and *patience* of hope;" and we learn that Paul's own ministry was appointed "unto *obedience of faith*" among all the nations.

¶ II. *Liberty in Christ Not to be Perverted into Licentiousness, but Maintained through Walking by the Spirit and Crucifying the Flesh. v. 13–26.*

1. True use of Christian freedom=For ye, brethren, were called for freedom; (A) only use not your freedom for an occasion to the flesh, (B) but through love be servants one to another. 13.

2. Scriptural enforcement of this injunction=For the whole law is fulfilled in one word, even in this; Thou shalt love thy neighbour as thyself. 14.

3. Consequence of the neglect of this duty held up as a warning=(A) But if you bite and devour one another, (B) take heed that you be not consumed one of another. 15.

4. The only way to avoid this result=But I say, (A) Walk by the spirit, (B) and you shall not fulfil the lust of the flesh. 16.

5. Explanatory reason=For (A) the flesh lusts against the Spirit, (B) and the Spirit against the flesh; (A B) for these are contrary the one to the other; 17.

6. Consequence=that ye may not do the things that ye would.

7. Method of avoiding this result=(A) But if you are led by the Spirit, (B) you are not under the law. 18.

8. Specification of the evils resulting from a failure to follow this leading=Now the works of the flesh are manifest, (A) which are these, (a) fornication, uncleanness, lasciviousness, (b) idolatry, sorcery, (c) enmities, strife, jealousies, wraths, (d) factions, divisions, heresies, envyings, (e) drunkenness, revellings, (B) and such like; 19-21.

9. Consequence of fulfilling these lusts of the flesh=of the which I forewarn you, even as I did forewarn you, that they who practice such things shall not inherit the kingdom of God. 21.

10. Description of the virtues to which the Spirit leads in contrast with those evils=But the fruit of the Spirit is love, joy, peace, longsuffering, kindness, goodness, faithfulness, meekness, temperance: 22, 23.

11. The character of these virtues as the direct opposite of unlawful carnal works=against such there is no law. 23.

12. Ground of this spiritual mode of life=And they that are of Christ Jesus have crucified the flesh with the passions and lusts thereof. 24.

13. Consequent exhortation=If we live by the Spirit, (A) by the Spirit let us also walk. (B) Let us not be vainglorious, (a) provoking one another, (b) envying one another. 25, 26.

Queries.

(1). How the love of one's neighbour regarded as the fulfilment of the law toward him? 14. *Cf.* Rom. xiii. 10.

(2). How the warfare between the flesh and the Spirit related to the failure of Christians to do what they would? 17.

It is absurd to suppose that this failure is either humanly or divinely designed by such warfare. The connecting conjunction in this passage (*hina*) evidently points simply to the *result* of the warfare to which reference is made. It is one of the many passages that clearly disproves the theory of Meyer, Alford and others, that the conjunction here used *always* denotes purpose or design. Feeling the force of this passage as indicating simply a consequence, Alford concedes that "this *is* the result" but he argues that "more is expressed by *hina*." And what reason does he adduce? "The necessity of supposing an ecbatic meaning for *hina* in theology is obviated by remembering that, with God, results are all purposed." This is simply urging a false theological opinion in support of a defective definition of a Greek term!

(3). How "not under the law" when "led by the Spirit"? 18. *Cf.* ver. 23 and I. Tim. i. 9.

(4). What the import of the original term corresponding to the word "revellings"? 21.

"Jovial festivity with music and dancing." (Liddell and Scott.) And, in truth, nothing more fully exemplifies the thought expressed by our word "revelling" than the sensual tide of feeling engendered by the vulgar and unholy embrace of the modern waltz. The gross immorality resulting in a multitude of cases justifies the description just given as expressing the true nature of this practice.

¶ III.   *The Service of Love Which is Due to Those Who are Beset with Infirmities and Temptations. vi. 1–5.*

1. Duty to the erring=Brethren, (A) even if a man be overtaken in any trespass, (B) you who are spiritual, restore such a one in a spirit of meekness; 1.

2. Caution to the Spiritual themselves=looking to thyself, lest thou also be tempted.

3. Sympathy for those under trials enjoined=(A) Bear you one another's burdens, (B) and so fulfil the law of Christ. 2.

4. Condemnation of self-conceit as inconsistent with the discharge of this duty=For if a man thinks himself to be something, when he is nothing, he deceives himself. 3.

5. Consequent duty of humble self-knowledge to avoid imaginary superiority on account of another's fault=(A) But let each man prove his own work, (B) and then shall he have his glorying (a) in regard of himself alone, (b) and not of his neighbour. 4.

6. Ground of this obligation=For each man shall bear his his own burden. 5.

Queries.

(1).   Contextual force of the word "spiritual" in ver. 1?

(2).   What, in the nature of the case, is the relation of the duty here enjoined to disciplinary action?

(3).   Reconcile ver. 2 with ver. 5.
Notice the immediate connection of each.

¶ IV.   *Exhortation to the Maintenance of Christian Teachers and to Beneficence in General. vi. 6–10.*

1.   Duty to religious instructors=But let him who is taught in the word communicate unto him who teaches in all good things. 6.

2.   Caution against the mistake of supposing that all is well regardless of duty=(A) Be not deceived; (B) God is not mocked: 7.

3.   Justification of this statement by reference to a divine law in nature=(A) for whatsoever a man sows, (B) that shall he also reap.

4.   Spiritural application=(A) For he that sows unto his own flesh shall of the flesh reap corruption; (B) but he that sows unto the Spirit shall of the Spirit reap eternal life. 8.

5.   Admonitory enforcement of the condition of reaping eternal life=(A) And let us not be weary in well-doing: (B) for in due season we shall reap, if we faint not. 9.

6.   Hortatory conclusion=So then, as we have opportunity, (A) let us work that which is good toward all men, (B) and especially toward those who are of the household of faith. 10.

¶ V.   *Final Reference to the Judaizers. vi. 11–18.*

1.   His interest in the Galatians indicated by the manner of composing the Epistle=See with how large letters I have written unto you with mine own hand. 11.

2.   Exposure of the Judaizers on the other hand as destitute of any real interest in them=As many as desire to make a fair show in the flesh, (A) they compel you to be circumcised; (B) only that they may not be persecuted for the cross of Christ. 12.

3.   Further description of their sinister motives and feelings =(A) For not even they who receive circumcision do themselves

keep the law ; (B) but (a) they desire to have you circumcised, (b) that they may glory in your flesh. 13.

4. Indication on the other hand of his own ground of glory-ing=But far be it from me to glory, save in the cross of our Lord Jesus Christ, (A) through which the world has been crucified unto me, (B) and I unto the world. 14.

5. Explanatory reason=(A) For neither is circumcision anything, (A²) nor uncircumcision, (B) but a new creature. 15.

6. Prayer for those who seek this high end=And as many as shall walk by this rule, (A) peace be upon them, and mercy, (B) and upon the Israel of God. 16.

7. Expression of his desire for exemption from further annoyance from adversaries=From henceforth let no man trouble me : 17.

8. Proof of his worthiness to this end=for I bear branded on my body the marks of Jesus.

9. Benediction=The grace of our Lord Jesus Christ be with your spirit, brethren. Amen. 18.

Queries.

(1). Comparing ver. 14 with iii. 13 what is seen to be the twofold power of the cross of Christ?

(2). As glorying only in the cross, in what striking contrast does the apostle stand not only with the stumbling Jew and the captious Greek of old (I. Cor. i. 23), but equally with the super-cilious rationalist of our day?

(3). Comparing the significant formula in ver. 15 with the same as slightly varied in v. 6, and again in I. Cor. vii. 19, what relation is discernible between "faith working through love," "the keeping of the commandments of God," and the process of the "new creation" through Christ?

*9 781584 270744 *